Living

Myth

[L.J. "Tess" Tessier]

Youngstown State University

Kendall Hunt

publishing company

Cover image © Shutterstock, Inc.

Kendall Hunt
publishing company

www.kendallhunt.com
Send all inquiries to:
4050 Westmark Drive
Dubuque, IA 52004-1840

CONTENTS

To my mother, for teaching me to love these stories
and to Tara, for helping me live them.

You need chaos in your soul
To give birth to a dancing star.
Nietzsche

PREFACE

What a piece of work is a man, how noble in reason, how
infinite in faculties, in form and moving how express and
admirable, in action how like an angel, in apprehension how like
a god! The beauty of the world, the paragon of animals ...
W. Shakespeare

What is it about being human? The opening quote is from *Hamlet* (Act II, scene 2), and the depressed Dane did not have a very positive attitude toward people, so he was probably being sarcastic. However, this view of human beings as the crown of creation has a very large following. Some religious traditions hold that the whole of creation exists as a gift from the divine to God's ultimate masterpiece: the human.

What makes us so special? There are several human characteristics that experts cite as indicating human superiority. Our abilities to reason and to communicate are often mentioned, but perhaps we do not come off quite as well as we think. Human beings are the only species of mammal that will knowingly foul our own food and water supply, so perhaps we are not quite as smart as we think we are. Though our communication methods are extraordinarily complex, bees and ants certainly communicate more effectively than we do.

When I think about the wonders of being human, I am most impressed by our sense of humor and our capacity for music. Other animals certainly play and enjoy themselves, but we tell better jokes. And although a nightingale can create a splendid sound, she can't sing Mozart.

Many point to a trait that may be distinctly human (although there's evidence that other species experience it to some extent). That is reflexivity, the capacity to view ourselves as both subject and object, to be self-aware. This is, of course, extraordinary. We are able to ponder our own thoughts and actions, to develop a conscience, and to reflect upon our various roles in life. It comes with a price, however, and that price is also one that the earth must pay unless we reach beyond our self-study to practice more interrelatedness with other species.

Perhaps the wonder of being human is not so much in what we think but in the way that we think. Humans are meaning-giving creatures, and the basic units of our consciousness and our thought processes are symbols. In fact, we cannot think without symbols. They are the basic building blocks of human thought, and symbol making is a primary activity of human life. At the most basic level, then, symbols are what humans utilize in order to formulate and communicate meaning, and our capacity to use symbols reaches far beyond the basic.

This is not, however, primarily a book about symbols. It is a book about stories—the most powerful and significant stories people have ever told. The key that unlocks these stories, however, is a form of symbol that is uniquely human—the *metaphor*. In fact, rhetorical analysis of human thought and speech suggests that the cognitive structures of human thought are metaphorical. Joseph Campbell, certainly one of the most renowned scholars of myth, recognizes metaphor as the central focus of all myth. In fact, from his perspective, myths are metaphors.

Campbell also emphasizes one particular theme as the earliest and most foundational of mythic stories. From his point of view, the facets of meaning revealed in the motif of the hero's journey serve as the basis for all mythic narratives. In fact, the hero's journey is actually the story of human life. This theme also provides the focal point for this study of symbol, myth, and ritual. Exploration of myth invites us on a hero's journey of our own, from creation through the processes of naming, interacting with the divine, and encountering obstacles, through death, transformation, and rebirth. These aspects of the adventure form the outline of this book.

It would perhaps be helpful to set out here what will not be found in this text. I have not included the complete text of the myths to which I refer, although guidance will be provided to where these stories can be found. I have not included detailed historical or cultural information such as would be appropriate in an anthropological approach. Furthermore, no attempt has been made here to discuss in detail the causes that might lie beneath the formation of these myths (such as attempts to explain natural phenomena, psychological expressions, etc.). This book is about the meanings and themes to be found in the stories themselves.

There are certainly scholars who would object that these stories cannot even be considered separately from their cultural context, and to a certain extent this is true. Whether we know about them or not, all of these stories have origins, cultural contexts and histories. They affected the cultures that told them and were in turn affected by those cultures. A great deal of scholarship exists surrounding all of the themes, cultures, and theories discussed in this text. Therefore, this book can only serve as a diving board into the stories and the ways in which human beings might relate to them. Once one chooses to swim in these waters, there are many currents to explore. Where I can, I will suggest resources for more extensive exploration.

Our vastly expanded access to information and research is both a boon and a barrier to consideration of these myths. Human beings are both social and astoundingly creative. Myths are both ancient and orally transmitted. Put all this together, and these mythic traditions are extremely fluid. For every version of a god's adventures, there is a variant from some other time and place. Every god and hero that rises up from the past goes by many names, becomes associated with various cultures, and interacts with those cultures in various ways. Whether the traditions related to various deities are identical with, related to, or derived from other traditions is always a matter of some debate.

Scholars deal with all this contrasting and sometimes conflicting information in various ways. They may debate about which versions are more original or authentic. They may discuss the original interpretations or functions of these myths or how they fit into the practices of various cults. They may also choose a particular version of a myth to analyze or to illustrate a particular perspective.

This text recognizes that there are always variants in ancient traditions, and where these differences provide additional insight, I have attempted to include at least some reference to them. However, in no way do I claim that every (or any) story I discuss here is the original or only version. I take the function of the mythic in human life very seriously, and the assumption that the themes and meanings found in ancient traditions are powerful truths still valid and beneficial in contemporary culture is perhaps the most basic presupposition I have made here. With this perspective in mind, the accuracy of a particular version of each myth is not as significant as the meanings we can derive from it.

The works of Mircea Eliade and Joseph Campbell have certainly influenced my own study of myth, and no discussion of this topic could possibly be complete without them. However, this text is not an attempt to build upon prior theoretical positions. More specifically, I am not convinced that any specific type of myth, whether cosmogony or hero's journey, serves as a "monomyth"—an original prototype from which all other forms of myth derive. Though this text is loosely structured around the theme of a hero's journey, my own view of this motif differs in many ways from that of Joseph Campbell. Rather than basing this exploration on any prior work, I find this motif to be a helpful and provocative approach to exploring some of the myriad paths that lead us into mythic realms.

The impetus behind this text is perhaps best revealed by its title. Though the origin of many of these tales predates recorded history, the motifs they consider, the secrets they reveal, are as alive now as they have been throughout human history. Perhaps no culture or language is ever truly "dead." If the past were only the past, there would likely be no point in poking about in it. Myths offer us so much more than a look backward, and this text seeks not so much to study what these stories were but to consider how they live on in us and where they might lead us.

Even in the early stages of scholarship in the field, some extremely important anthropological and analytical work on myths, symbols and rituals was done by women (Mead, von Franz, and others). The best-known scholars, however, are male. Though scholars like Frazer, Freund, Doty, Long, Eliade, and Campbell have contributed massively to scholarship in this area, their focus, not surprisingly, has influenced developments in the field in favor of male figures and patriarchal interpretations. Joseph Campbell, for example, has been strongly critiqued for the obvious sexist perspective in some of his work. Because of its popularity, based in part on the Bill Moyers interviews, this bias is especially troubling. Though critique of this bias is beyond the scope of this book, I have intentionally focused some of my discussion on myths involving female deities and heroes and on alternative perspectives challenging some of the better-known traditional views.

Study of myth does not seem to me to have as much impact on contemporary academic work as it has in the past. Although this area of study typically has a place in the curricula of anthropology and literature programs, the impact of the mythic is not as much of a consideration in contemporary life and scholarship. If I believed that these narratives are merely curious and arcane artifacts from the distant past, this sidelining of the mythic would make sense. However, it is my belief that mythic narratives and the rituals that bring them to life are part of what it is to be human, and that our intellectual and psychological lives are starved without some exercising of the mythic imagination.

While some scholars in religious studies may consider studies of myth and ritual to be somewhat peripheral, their impact on contemporary culture is undisputed. The academy may focus elsewhere, but many writers, playwrights, film directors, and creators of video and computer games have a better understanding of what engages the human imagination. One need only consider the impact of a few narratives to realize how deeply we are drawn to the mythic: The Lord of the Rings, Star Wars, The Matrix, and Harry Potter, not to mention all manner of monsters, continue to draw us into their magical world, hungry to see ourselves again reflected in these mythic mirrors. Those who would remove the mythic power from spirituality may react suspiciously to the symbolic images in these tales, but lines still form around the block to see films with mythic content.

With this perspective in mind, I have included in my discussion some consideration of the connections we in contemporary culture may experience when reflecting upon these narratives. These observations are, of course, somewhat skewed by my own personality and experiences, but it is my hope that others will find observations here to which they can relate. Though I have included some consideration of ways in which ancient cultures interacted with these mythic traditions, I have not focused as much on past cultures and their interpretations of these themes.

As mentioned above, the structure of this book is based very loosely on the mythic cycle itself. After a general discussion of the terms and concepts involved in the study of symbols, myths, and rituals, the following chapters track the stages of the cycle from creation to rebirth and return. In the final chapter, I have included a discussion of some of the ways ancient myths function in contemporary culture. At the end of each chapter, I have included study questions, discussion questions, and information about where complete versions of the myths mentioned in each chapter may be found.

ACKNOWLEDGEMENTS

To acknowledge and thank all who have helped can only be too short or too long. I have opted for the short version and hope that all not specifically named will know that they are included and how much they are appreciated.

I have in my possession a copy of an academic paper entitled "Leviathan," by Ronald M. Huntington. Dr. Huntington gave it to me when I was a student in his Myth, Symbol, and Ritual course at Chapman College in the City of Orange, California. The pages are now soft and yellowed, since that exchange took place about three decades ago. Much of the design for my own course, especially in my early years of teaching, I owe directly to Ron Huntington. He not only brought ancient myths to life for me, but also introduced me to a new way of thinking about creation (and chaos) that, perhaps more than anything else, launched me on my own academic adventure. Ron took his journey to another level in 1994, and I hope that wherever he is now, he still gets to play the organ and direct the choir.

None of us could do what we do without mentors, and the scholar-pathfinders who traveled before me have also enriched my own academic journey beyond measure. I wish to particularly thank Christine Downing, both for her inspirational work and for her incredibly helpful support of this project.

Many voices echo in these pages, and not all of them are ancient ones. Students in my Myth, Symbol and Ritual course over the past 20 years have raised questions, offered insights, and shared their own visions of these ancient narratives, adding to my own understanding (and confusion) in ways too numerous to mention. They are always my most treasured reference. Students taking the course in 2010-11 were especially helpful in the writing of this text.

I am extraordinarily fortunate to have colleagues in the Philosophy and Religious Studies Department at Youngstown State University who are unfailingly supportive, and even celebratory of my work. I am grateful to every one of them. I especially wish to thank Department Chair Bruce Waller for going out of his way to support this project, from helping me find time to work, to forming a one-man cheering squad. I am also grateful to Chris Bache for sharing the vision and finding the perfect title.

My research assistant, Amanda Benchwick, has been extremely helpful in tracking down sources and helping me find answers to questions that neither of us saw coming. She was also helpful beyond measure in constructing the glossary and other reference material. Candace Lev was also very helpful in locating some critical material.

The staff at Kendall Hunt has been wonderfully efficient, supportive, and gracious to me. Thanks especially to Scott Perrine for believing in this project and carrying it forward and to Amanda Smith for keeping me on track and putting the whole thing together. I am quite certain that most textbook authors do not get to present their work in texts that are this beautiful, so I also very much thank the design team for their terrific work.

My family, my friends—if I tried to name all of you who have helped me so much over the years, I do not know that I would ever find an end to the list. You know who you are, especially the dragons among you.

It is unfathomably impossible to express my gratitude to Tara McKibben. Fortunately, I believe she understands. I would also like to very much thank all the four-leggeds that share our household. Fortunately, those of you with animals will understand.

It is beyond my pay grade to offer sufficient thanks to all the gods and monsters. I feel them hovering around me now—and laughing.

[chapter]

WHAT OTHERWISE
COULD NOT BE SAID

We are symbols, and inhabit symbols; workman, work, and tools, words and things, birth and death, all are emblems; but we sympathize with the symbols, and, being infatuated with the economical uses of things, we do not know that they are thoughts.

Ralph Waldo Emerson[1]

Too often, the study of symbols in relationship to myths and rituals is framed only in terms of ancient narratives and traditions, recalling cultures now either extinct or very remote, and comparing them to our contemporary way of thinking. Sometimes these past traditions are viewed with nostalgia, sometimes with disdain, but the immediacy of the impact these forces have upon us is rarely discussed.

Symbols carry us through every human communication. Myths reconnect us to ourselves, to one another and to the sacred. Rituals enable us to create the universe anew. These concepts are not relics of the past. They still support our deepest human interactions, and understanding them enables us to better understand our world and ourselves.

Since it is our intention to demonstrate the living power of symbols, myths, and rituals, too many technical definitions will not enhance our discussion. However, before we explore their extraordinary power, we must understand what they are and how they work.

[symbols]

Symbols are the basic building blocks of human thought, but they do more than provide structure for our thinking. We not only use symbols to create meaning, but also to communicate, to learn and to classify knowledge, and to express emotion. The English word "symbol" is etymologically derived from the Greek *syn* (together) and *ballein* (to throw), literally to throw together. Therefore, a symbol is anything that represents another thing, due to the associations we make through conceptual connection or perceived resemblance.

Symbols are more than mere records or copies of reality. German philosopher Ernst Cassirer observed that symbolic forms are not just imitations but "*organs* of reality," since it is only through symbols that we can perceive and intellectually apprehend the world. In the human mind, "only that can be visible which has some definite form; but every form of existence has its source in some peculiar way of seeing, some intellectual formulation and intuition of meaning."[2]

While non-human animals can and do single out objects according to their impulses and instincts, these objective forms last only while the animals' impulses are directly stimulated. Only human symbolic expression contains the possibility of considering these forms in relationship to past experiences and future possibilities, "because it is only by symbols that distinctions are not merely *made,* but *fixed* in consciousness."[3]

Following Cassirer, Suzanne Langer notes that the need to symbolize, to create meanings, and to apply these meanings to our sensory experience, is a basic and pervasive human need. Symbolism is "the recognized key to that mental life which is characteristically human and above the level of sheer animality."[4] For humans, then, and only for humans, symbolization is a fundamental process of the mind, a primary activity that goes on continuously. [5]

In analyzing the way that symbols work to convey meaning, scholars have distinguished between the *signifier* (what we perceive), the *signified* (the meaning we give to the perception), and *signification* (the relationship between the two). For example, a red rose (the signifier) may be understood as a symbol of love (the signified). The relationship or association between the rose and the concept of love is its signification.

An enormous and exciting field of study has grown up around the various ways that humans construct and utilize signs and symbols. Though these discussions add much to our understanding of human communication, we cannot include them all here. However, a few key distinctions are essential to understanding the ways in which we assign meaning to symbols.

Though the term "symbol" can be used as a blanket term for anything that serves to convey meaning, many scholars have suggested a breakdown of the general term into signals, signs, and symbols. *Signals* express the relationship between signifier and signified as active and causal. They convey specific information directed toward inciting action or directing behavior. Although humans make extensive use of signals such as traffic lights and hand signals, animals also make use of signals to warn, arouse, and even to direct traffic (such as wolf howls during a hunt).

A sign tends to have a single meaning, since the signifier and the signified are very closely related. When we see a pillar of smoke rising into the sky, we understand that a fire is burning without ever seeing the flames. Cultures also develop sign systems such as codes in which a particular mark or sound may stand for a particular letter. A blind individual can read Braille because each raised grouping always stands for the same particular character.

What distinguishes symbols from signals and signs is their complexity. Symbols have multiple meanings, and their associations are much more fluid, layered, and multi-faceted. Their references are typically ambiguous and abstract. Symbolic signification (the relationship between signifier and signified) may express an analogy between things from different contexts that are normally unconnected. Beyond direct connections between objects and the words we use to describe them, symbols enable us to develop an extraordinarily complex web of meanings. We can extend our frame of reference from a specific symbol to its characteristics and associations. We can launch our imaginations from a single image to a profound philosophical concept.

One distinction among symbols that has become commonplace is that between what Langer called *discursive* symbols and those she termed *presentational*. Discursive symbols are singular and discrete. We must experience them in a certain arrangement in order to determine their meaning. Their organizational system is fairly simple, since the symbols appear one after another like clothes on a clothesline. The most obvious of these symbols is written language. If the letters of a word or a sentence are scrambled, we must mentally put them into the right order before we can understand their meaning.

Presentational symbols, on the other hand, must be perceived as a whole before we can realize their meanings. The elements of a painting cannot be read left to right or top to bottom. Rather, we must "take in" all of the various aspects of the painting in order to obtain the fullest possible meaning. Likewise, though the individual notes are discrete and linear, a symphonic phrase cannot be understood apart from the whole symphony. Presentational symbols cannot be directly translated. The components of presentational symbols have very complex relationships, and each component can only be understood as part of a whole.

Another important symbolic distinction is between those that are arbitrary or conventional and those that seem somehow to participate in or point to their meanings. Arbitrary symbols have no specific relationship between signified and signifier, except that some person or persons have decided that "x" should mean or stand for "y." The letters used in algebraic equations are an obvious example. Culturally determined symbols are obviously dependent on context, and the same symbol may have different meanings both within and among cultures. Apples, for example, are associated in the United States with teachers, especially as gifts, although there is nothing specific about the apple itself that leads us to think of teachers.

Other symbols seem to actively participate in their own meanings, usually by bearing a significant likeness or resemblance to what they symbolize. Caution is required, however. Even when there is a clear connection between the symbol and its meaning, cultures still interpret these symbols in many ways.

Where symbols do in some way participate in or point toward their meanings, these resemblances take various forms. *Iconic* symbols are typically geometric relationships. They are pictures or images of objects or concepts that may range from the very concrete (a realistic portrait) to much more abstract images such as maps and graphs.

The resemblance between signified and signifier may also be expressed through more abstract similarities such as physical characteristics, function, or conceptual similarities. For example, *metaphors* imply comparison between entities emerging from divergent cultural contexts and rely on a sensory resemblance or conceptual similarity.

The power of a metaphor lies in its capacity to carry the mind far beyond the initial image. The feminist theologian Nelle Morton illustrates this "kindling of the imagination" through use of her own abstract symbols:

> An image cannot become metaphoric until it is on its way—like a meteor. Where it explodes, or how soon, when it burns out, how long or how far it journeys, are unknowns. … [W]hether you stay by to its finished action, whether your imagination is such it can follow the process and participate in the surprise, the new reality, is another matter. The final metaphoric action is always a surprise, for the new reality it ushers in is like a revelation.[6]

Metaphors come alive as our inner symbolic world meets the image and completes it. Since each individual mind develops its own unique symbolic framework, and since each individual symbolic world is different from all others, the action of a metaphor is always dynamic. Each experience of any metaphor is unique.

Metaphors are the symbolic forms that carry the meanings we find in myths, and insights about their function have enabled scholars to interpret ancient stories and scriptures with greater depth. The way that metaphors function in myth will be discussed in the following section.

Some symbols are so extraordinary that they belong in a category of their own. These are the *hierophanic* symbols that have the unique capacity to incorporate the sacred and to bring it to life. Not only do these images provide us with information about our relationship with the divine, but also they have the capacity to *manifest* the sacred—to bring the divine right here, with us, absolutely present. The function of these unique symbols also will be more fully elaborated in the following discussion of myth.

It is a tribute to our amazing and uniquely human symbolic capacity that we have the ability to communicate these complex and individual symbolic journeys to one another. At more abstract levels, symbols allow us to express what we could not otherwise articulate. Contradictory impulses and emotions can be brought together. Oppositions between reason and emotion, nature and culture, sacred and profane can be overcome. Charles Long observes the power of religious symbols to integrate diverse meanings into one totality, "thus expressing in a profound and intense manner the paradoxical structure of that which is ultimately real."[7]

Obviously, the more abstract the associations and resemblances between signifer and signified, the wider the range of interpretations. Victor Turner observes a characteristic of symbols he calls *multivocality.* Because they demonstrate ambiguity and complexity of association, a wide range of groups and individuals might relate to the same symbol in a variety of ways.[8] What seems to be a clear association in one culture may not be so obvious somewhere else.

The term *swastika,* for example, is Sanskrit and means something like lucky or auspicious. It is an ancient shape that appears naturally in square-shaped basket weaving, and its design, an equilateral cross with its arms bending at right angles, resulted in cultural associations with the cross and the wheel. Eventually, of course, the swastika became one of the most loathed images in the world because of its association with the Nazi regime. However, it meant something entirely different and much more noble when it was incorporated into the sand paintings of Tibet or worked into the hem of a Chinese emperor's robe.

Furthermore, the meanings that we arrange are affected by the unusual way that humans perceive. In the 1920's, a group of German psychologists called *gestalt perception* theorists made some observations about the ways in which humans interact with their environment that enhanced our understanding of how human perception is organized.

Among their observations is a phenomenon called "figure-ground" perception. They noted that humans seem to have an innate tendency to perceive one specific aspect of what we perceive as "figure" (the foreground) and the rest as "ground" (background). The figure need not be an object. Rather, the term refers to any perception (a sound, an activity, even a thought) that becomes the primary object of our focus.[9] More contemporary studies of human perception such as those conducted by Earl Miller, a neuroscientist at MIT, suggest that, in spite of our penchant for "multitasking," we cannot, in fact, perceive more than one or two figures at a time. However, humans have the ability to toggle from one to another at an incredibly rapid pace.[10] While our perceptions move constantly from one figure to another, we perceive the environment, not in fractional images, but as a whole composed of all the figures of which we are aware and their backgrounds. This process is perpetual, and changes very rapidly. As we assign meanings to objects and events, our minds apply organizing principles that smooth out the rough edges of our perception, and put things together into a "whole" perception. Additionally, our minds constantly adjust our understanding according to the relationships we perceive among the figures. Behind the principles of gestalt is the assumption that the world we experience is always, to some extent, meaningfully organized.

We learn not just from the things we literally perceive, but also from the relationships among them. Our internal processes always affect our external perceptions. What we have experienced in the past, our network of needs, values, and beliefs, all affect our choice of figures, and the meanings we ascribe to them. We constantly integrate our figures into the meaning that we have already constructed. Gestalt theory holds that the meaning we associate with a figure is critical to the ways in which we associate that figure with its background. All the perceptions and associated meanings that form our experience are our own background. Our past understanding of ourselves, others, and the world around us constantly informs our current perceptions and the meanings we give them.

myth

Human beings may be hard wired for narrative. Not only are our brains designed to think symbolically, but recent studies regarding the structure of our thinking also suggest that our entire conceptual framework is fundamentally metaphorical. We use the power of the metaphor to bring reason and imagination together, to comprehend partially what we can never understand fully—our emotions, our artistic and moral values, and our spirituality. [11]

The first story at the core of our thinking is always our own story. We attach our memories, the story of where we have been, to the present in an unfolding narrative that not only tells us what is happening, but also helps us know who we are. That narrative then extends into the future as we build the story from what we next intend to eat to what we plan as our most ambitious and far reaching goals. We are comfortable with stories. They are organic to us.

In contemporary culture, the term "myth" is typically used to refer to a common belief that is not true. However, the expression, "It's just a myth," indicates a serious loss of connection and identity in our culture. This notion that myth is false completely misses the vital connection to story upon which a healthy mind and a sturdy culture depend.

To begin with, then, myths are true. They are fundamentally, eternally, ultimately true. The key to understanding that myths are true is to realize the sorts of truths that myths tell and the language that myths use to communicate.

These mythic truths are our most profound guides to understanding ourselves as individuals, as communities, and as cultures. First, they help us understand who we are. As Karen Armstrong points out, myths are true because they are *effective*—they enable us to find a psychological and spiritual path and guide us toward effective action along that path.[12] However, this issue of identity is more than an individual matter. Identity is a relational concept. We do not really know who we are until we come into contact with others, and our identity, our personhood, is formed in relation. Therefore, myths also tell us truths about our most fundamental relationships—first with ourselves, but also with those we love, with those who surround us, with all living things, with our planet, and finally with the entire cosmos. Myths are always about these relationships. Many scholars point out that myths are also about origins—they help us know who we are by helping us understand where we started and where we have been.

In order to access these truths and unfold the secrets of myth, we must also understand the language of myth. All language is, of course, symbolic, but the symbolic language of myth is of a different order. Joseph Campbell observes that the living metaphors of myth deliver not only ideas, but also a sense of actual participation in the world. "Indeed, the first and most essential service of a mythology is this one, of opening the mind and heart to the utter wonder of all being."[13] Transcending the false idea of "material things as things-in-themselves," mythic metaphors have both psychological and metaphysical connotations. "By way of this dual focus the psychologically significant feature of any local social order, environment, or supposed history can be transformed through myth into transparencies revelatory of transcendence."[14] Campbell's work forcefully illustrates that the symbols in myth carry their truths metaphorically, pointing beyond themselves to greater underlying truths. Because of this language, myths have the capacity to reach beyond ordinary narrative and to communicate what could not otherwise be expressed. They extend beyond our rationality and take us places we could not otherwise reach.

Paul Ricoeur's well-known definition of myth provides additional insight into the power of myth in human culture. He describes myth as

> ... a traditional narration which relates to events that happened at the beginning of time and which has the purpose of providing grounds for the ritual actions of men [sic] of today and, in a general manner, establishing all the forms of action and thought by which man understands himself in his [sic] world. [15]

If myths just gave us key information about identity and relationships, that alone would be a great gift, but the functions of myth go beyond this. They are more than blueprints. They are complex plans that tell us not just what is there and how it came to be, but also how the structures should continue and be maintained. They are our guides to ritual, to organization of our lives, to the structure of our cultures, to confronting the most absolute human issues: birth, love, conflict, and death.

Doty notes that myths are never concerned with the trivial. Since they involve the most central and essential aspects of a culture's perspectives, behaviors, and attitudes, they are "originary." That is, their capacity to embody the ideas, values, and models of the heroic and supreme extends their effectiveness from generation to generation. Myths are not so much religious as foundational material, relating the divine to the "experienced conditions of human existence."[16]

Another facet of myth is its capacity to overcome oppositions. As our intellect collides with our emotional impulses, as our emotions become entangled or travel in opposite directions at once, we need some way to overcome the duality and to reconcile the apparent paradox. Because of the power of complex symbols discussed above, myths can bring these conflicts into resolution, even into reconciliation. Water may symbolize creation and destruction. The human heart is a symbol of both courage and betrayal. Kali the Destroyer is also Mother Kali, life giver and protector. Cupid's arrows cause "sweet wounds."

To summarize, myths point to ultimate truths about identity and relationships, and provide guidelines for the structure and organization of our lives and our cultures. They also bring together the complex elements of the psyche and assist us to reach for deeper meanings.

This understanding of myth helps to illuminate the power of sacred stories. Of course, we can take the position that the sacred stories of our own traditions are "true," and those of other cultures are "just myths." However, the literal truth of these narratives, whether written into scripture or carried forward in other ways, may be the least significant issue to consider. These sacred narratives are true because they reveal the divine and, through the power of hierophanic symbols, assist humanity in making direct contact with the power of the sacred. The well-known cultural historian and religious scholar, Thomas Berry, claims that myths not only provide us with "the interpretative patterns of our existence," but also link us to the universe and to the sacred. Our contemporary critical analysis and pragmatic realism have cut us off from the world of the sacred, once available to humanity through the mythic imagination, and left us suffocating in "consumerism and the excitement over the instant communication of the trivial." In order to recover meaning, we must recover the sacred through "a return to the depths of our own being."[17]

origins

The study of myth draws us into an encounter with many mysteries. One such puzzle has to do with the fact that myths do not come to us fresh from a publisher with author and title. Where do myths originate? In fact, the question is a bit misleading. Perhaps the best way to approach the question is to consider the similarity between myths and dreams. Where do dreams originate? Although we have a vague sense that dreams come to us in our sleep from a psychological location that is not ordinarily accessible, we cannot point to an aspect of our thought or our personality and say, "This is my subconscious." Likewise, we cannot point to a geographical or historical location as the birthplace of myth. Just as dreams come "up from down under,"[18] myths emerge from ancient cultures, move for an unknown time as oral traditions through various cultures, and eventually come to be "known" as recorded stories.

This is not to say that there are no myths emerging from later cultures or even contemporary "myths in the making." However, to reach a point where these stories have the power to bring ultimate reality into contact with human interactions, they must stew a bit in the subterranean juices of human cultures.

commonalities

Another mythic mystery derives from the observation that very similar myths appear in parts of the world far removed from one another. How is it that Tibetans and Navajo have very similar stories, and both traditions ritualize these narratives through sand paintings? Why do certain creation myths reiterate the same themes in so many different times and places? Although there are many speculations in the scholarship, a few theories seem particularly pertinent to understanding the nature of myth.

Some scholars have suggested that myths are similar because they share a common origin. For example, similar creation myths may stem from a common point and may initially have been based on actual historical events. Storytellers then retold these stories and carried them from place to place along migration routes. The differences among myths with common themes emerge because of the effects of time and local cultural circumstances.

However, theories based on common origins and migration patterns cannot account for all the similarities that we discover. We cannot trace every theme to its origin. Perhaps the similarities are more fundamental than sharing a common geographical source. Perhaps the source is within us, and these similarities have to do with the nature of being human.

We have discussed the structure of human thought and its dependence upon symbolic forms. All human brains obviously share some characteristics, and it is possible that our thought patterns are more biologically based than we realize. Perhaps certain symbolic structures just come with the territory.

Carl Jung suggested that by virtue of being human, we share certain inherited patterns or forms of thought that shape our perception of the world. These *archetypes* provide the ancient, unconscious source for many of our ways of thinking and acting. For Jung, these primitive forms are with us from the moment of birth and remain in the depths of our unconscious. In myths, these archetypes take the form of motifs that reoccur in different times and places. Jung connected these archetypes with his concept of the *collective unconscious,* the form of consciousness shared by humans that owes its existence, not to individual experience, but to heredity.

As humans, of course, we share a great deal more than genetics. Though climates and geographies vary widely, all humans interact with our environment and share certain needs and desires. We all live under the same sky and experience seasonal rhythms, the dangerous magnificence of earth, wind, and water, and the emotions and urges that accompany the human condition. In order to survive and thrive, we must develop the means to understand and interpret our surroundings. Perhaps our shared experiences and interactions cause us to symbolize the most significant aspects of our lives in similar ways.

the mythic world view

Most myths emerge from what might be called "primal" or "aboriginal" cultures. There are a number of opinions about what language should be used to describe the cultures that maintain a mythic worldview. The term "primitive" suggests that such cultures are prior to and less developed than "civilized" cultures. This term also suppresses our realization that a few such cultures still exist. The mythic imagination is not merely a relic of human evolution, now put behind us as we advance into a more "mature" worldview. Whatever term we apply, there are aspects of the mythic worldview that provide us with additional insight into the power and function of myth. Here, we will use "primal" to refer to the people and communities from whom the mythic worldview originated.

Though it is common practice to generalize about the activities and beliefs of primal people, a bit of caution is required. There are no generic aboriginal people, no paradigmatic tribes. Prior to the rising of those great cultures that came to dominate world history, primal people lived in various local communities with various climates, plant and animal communities, and types of terrain. Some hunted or farmed; some did not. Some wandered; some remained in one geographical location. Some communities were composed of only a few families. Some were composed of tens of thousands of people. There may once have been as many as two thousand separate and distinct cultures on the North American continent. Their mythologies also varied, affected by their local geography and social practices. However, just as some generalizations can be made about the rise of the so-called great religions, we can draw some tentative conclusions about the primal worldview.

To the extent that we can explore the differences between the mythic worldview and our contemporary views, a few significant elements help us to understand the realm of the mythic. Karen Armstrong notes that even the early Paleolithic cultures distinguished between what the Greeks would come to call *logos* and *mythos*. Logos is logical and pragmatic, focused on the outer world of objective observations and conclusions. Mythos, on the other hand, is emotional and imaginative, focused on the inner world of meaning and spirituality. In the ancient world, these realms were understood to be complementary. Though they belonged to separate spheres, humans needed both modes of thought.[19]

In the past, certain scholars assumed that literacy was the key sign of cultural advancement. The development of reading and writing indicated that a culture had "arrived" at a more mature social arrangement. However, it is interesting to note that some of the most culturally advanced nations, such as Japan, did not develop a written language until rather late in their historical development.

Literate cultures depend upon reading and writing not only to develop learning and explore it but also to maintain it in written records. However, this practice leads to dependence on the written record in order to have access to the past. For example, the writings of Aristotle were "lost" after the decline of Rome. In the ninth century, Arab scholars introduced Aristotle to the Islamic world in Arabic translations. From there, the work eventually found its way back into the Latin West in the thirteenth century. If these writings had not been preserved in some form, Western European philosophy would undoubtedly be very different from what it is today.

While written systems of cultural transmission are no more than 6,000 years old, oral traditions are as ancient as the human ability to speak. Without writing, oral traditions utilize spoken language and hearing to record and preserve their ideas and stories. These cultures have a unique access to the past through verbal memory. Oral narratives preserve the culture but also change over time, maintaining a cultural history that is both durable and dynamic.

Another characteristic of primal traditions lies in their perception of the relationship between the natural and the spiritual realms. A brief overview of the way that the great religious traditions developed historically will help to illustrate this point. Over approximately a 600-year period, between roughly 800 and 200 BCE, a cultural transformation took place that became so pivotal for the development of religions, that Karl Jaspers called it the "axial" age. In areas as distinct from one another as China, India, the Middle East, and Greece, people began to be more aware of human suffering and their own limitations. A sense of individual conscience developed and, along with it, a sense of being cut off or separated from the divine.

William James made the observation that all of the world religions that emerged in this period share at least one doctrine. They each observe a dis-ease, alienation between the human and the divine, and they each offer a solution. This observation is easy to over-simplify, and yet there is a sense in which Christianity can be understood as the salvation from sin, Buddhism as a pathway to the end of suffering, and Chinese religions as guides to the restoration of balance and harmony.

Although primal religions may maintain traditions and rituals to appease the gods or to communicate with the divine, there is no equivalent overarching alienation between the spirit world and the natural world. In fact, it is extremely difficult to understand where one ends and the other begins. The sacred can be understood as permeating the entire natural world, so one might say that the world is "soaked" in the sacred. The spirit world may be understood as underlying or supporting the natural world. In any case, the distance between the two, if it exists at all, is never great. Entities in the natural world have spiritual power that can be gathered, moved, or channeled. Shamans can make the journey between one realm and the other and be led by (and tricked by) spirits. This relatedness between the human, the natural, and the sacred extends into other relationships as well.

Primal cultures describe the relationship between humans and other living things in many different ways, but there is no great difference in kind between the human creature and the rest of the living world. "The earth for them is not of dust... but alive and a mother. The animals and plants, and all the peoples dwelling on her bosom, are her children, also regarded in a sacred way."[20] When the people of primal cultures observe that the eagle is their brother, or that the earth is their mother, they are speaking more literally than metaphorically. Certain cultures may describe themselves as directly descended from their totem animal and may see themselves as always in relationship and always guided by and protected by that animal. Likewise, humans are not elevated over other forms of life. As observers from Chief Seattle to Daniel Quinn have noted, primal people believe that humans belong to the earth, rather than making the claim that the earth belongs to humans.

There is one additional key to understanding the mythic worldview that may be the most important observation we can make about primal cultures. It is also the most startling difference between the world in which we live and the mythic world.

We are so familiar with the concept of a self, a body, a being as a discreet human entity that we find it almost impossible to understand the world in any other way. We think about identity, personality, and self. For many primal cultures, however, the body is the people, and the separation of an individual from that body is every bit as traumatic as separating a limb from an individual human body. For example, many African cultures ascribe to *ubuntu* or *botho,* the concept that a person is a person through other people, sometimes translated as "I am because we are." For these cultures, identity is not only relational, but also communal, and what happens to one individual in the community happens to the whole body of the people. Furthermore, the interconnectedness permeates the way that actions and events are understood. Your failure to respect the spirit of this tree is the reason that the rains have not come. My mistreatment of your brother causes a wound not just to you and your family, but also to the entire community, and the people must be made whole.

Underlying these specific differences, there is the deeper matter of overarching paradigms. How does the world work for the people of the myth? What are the patterns of life, the models of being?

It is not sufficient to observe that the mythical worldview is "cyclical," although that is certainly one key to understanding its patterns. Our view of the world within a historical framework gives us a time line, and a specifically linear way of understanding life and the world. There are beginnings and ends, progress and failure, starts and stops, creations and eschatons.

Primal people, living within, rather than on top of, their ecosystems, describe reality based on the world as they observe it. In the natural world, death is not the end of anything. Plants die, decay, and rot, and new life emerges fueled by the energy of that decay. New shoots spring forth from rotting trees, plants open under the ground, the moon shrinks and vanishes only to return in greater and greater splendor. The sun is daily destroyed and restored. Even our deceased relations come back to us in memories and dreams. Nothing is ever quite gone.

Scholars have sometimes criticized this mythic understanding as static and limited by its cyclical pattern. If the world constantly repeats itself, there is no development, no growth, no "progress." It was not until we developed an historical sense that we left behind this cyclical rut and developed great societies. However, even in the mythic cycles, each beginning is a new beginning, each creation of the world a new creation. This is not just a repetition of a primordial pattern, unraveling and reweaving the same fabric. Just as the soul reborn by baptism is a new soul, the day reborn at the sun's return is a new day. Therefore, the world does not merely repeat itself. It proceeds through a spiral of new beginnings.

————————————————[dreams]————————————————

These ancient patterns are not as far removed from contemporary human life and culture as they might seem. One of the most remarkable features of the mythic imagination is the strong similarity that can sometimes be found between the oldest stories rising from the primal past and the most recent stories told by our most advanced physicists and cosmologists. Perhaps the root of this similarity is to be found, not in the realm of cultural phenomena or scientific experimentation, but in that most personal of psychological realms—our dreams. Of all the forms of literature and story telling, only myths are so much like dreams. This is because myths serve the same function culturally that dreams serve personally. As Campbell notes, "... as the imagery of a dream is metaphorical of the psychology of its dreamer, that of a mythology is metaphorical of the psychological posture of the people to whom it pertains."[21]

The similarity between myths and dreams regarding their mysterious origins has already been discussed. Myths and dreams both communicate to us through the power of the metaphor, emerging from deep subliminal sources, relating significant truths to us in symbolic language.

Another consideration regarding the relationship between myths and dreams is that both experiences stand outside of any traditional understanding of time and space. In myths, as in dreams, the rules of time and space do not apply, and events can and do take place before the beginning; beings can instantly change from one condition, time frame, or nature to another. Male and female, before and after, now and then are up for grabs in the deepest realms of the human psyche.

Though it is not the case, as has sometimes been claimed, that vocabulary range necessarily reflects cultural values, [22] it may be misleading that, in English, we have only the one word "dream" to refer to all of our mental activities while sleeping. Perhaps if our vocabulary for dreaming were more complex, we might realize that there are various sorts of dreams that perform different psychological functions. Some dreams might be understood as simply sorting out the events of the day, while others might be seen to reveal important clues to the complex aspects of our personality, locked deep in the psyche and called to the surface while dreaming.

─────[ritual]─────

On the face of it, rituals are somewhat difficult to define. The word "ritual" derives from the Latin ritus, meaning religious or ceremonious activity. In the broadest sense, however, the term can be applied to all actions that have symbolic value. Rituals may be performed on specific occasions or at the discretion of an individual or a community. They may be performed singly or in groups, in reserved or arbitrary locations, in public or private, in secret or before audiences. A ritual may or may not be restricted to a certain group within a community and may or may not reflect the relationship between religious and social realms. When we narrow our perspective to rituals associated with myth and religion, a few general characteristics frequently apply. In addition to some association with the sacred, these rituals typically involve stylized or repetitive speech or action. They also typically take place in a time and space that is set apart for this purpose.

Catherine Bell notes that although there are many conflicting theories regarding the intrinsic qualities of ritual, most scholars refer to three primary characteristics: fixity, formality, and repetition. That is, rituals tend to be formal gatherings performed at fixed times and places and repeated at set intervals. Bell observes that these characteristics are frequent, but not universal, in the performance of ritual acts.[23]

The purposes of rituals also are varied. They may reflect religious obligations or ideals, or serve the spiritual or emotional needs of the practitioners. They may have cultural functions, such as strengthening of social bonds, social and moral education, or demonstration of rank, affiliation, or social status in the community. They may even be performed simply for pleasure.

Another issue that arises when attempting to define ritual is the distinction between ritual and habit or custom. There are several suggested technical distinctions, but our focus on ritual here will be on their importance in bringing symbolic or emotional values into actualization. Emile Durkheim points out that, when we wish to experience energies superior to those we ordinarily experience, we need some means to internalize these powers and make them a part of us. In order to do this, thought does not go far enough. It is necessary that we "place ourselves within their sphere of action, and that we set ourselves where we may best feel their influence; in a word, it is necessary that we act, and that we repeat the acts thus necessary every time we feel the need of renewing their effects."[24]

In a sense, patterns of activity are rituals rather than merely customs or habits when their performance brings their meanings to life and enriches human understanding.

Even with all of the wisdom that myths convey, there are certain truths that cannot be discovered by mere narration. Since myths are more guides to behavior than they are conveyors of fact, we must put them into practice in order to discover their truths.[25] Rituals break down the barrier between the listener and the story, and help make these narratives our own, pushing us "beyond the safe certainties of the familiar world into the unknown."[26]

This is myth as verb, as activity, as life itself. In performing these myths, we are not merely dramatizing them as if we were performing a play. In bringing them to life, we realize their active power. Rituals bring the sacred to us, they recreate the world, and they provide us with transformation and new life. "Reading a myth without the transforming ritual that goes with it is as incomplete an experience as simply reading the lyrics of an opera without the music."[27]

Rituals also provide direct links between humans, the natural world, and the sacred. As indicated above, primal people did not understand themselves to be on a higher level than other forms of life. Killing other animals for food, shelter, or protection meant destroying a friend or relation. Ceremonial activities appeased the spirits and honored them for laying down their lives so that people could live. From the earliest discoveries about human culture, we find that people lived their stories through ritual. Thomas Berry powerfully evokes the way in which rituals brought our earlier ancestors into direct contact with the powers of the universe:

> A pervasive religious rapport with the spirit powers of the natural world developed, and ritual enabled humans to enter into the grand liturgy of the universe. Seasonal renewal ceremonies brought humans into the rhythms of the solar cycle and the renewing splendor of the Earth.[28]

Religious rituals are inextricably bound to religious symbols and concepts.

As Clifford Geertz expresses it, the moods and motivations that sacred symbols generate, and the beliefs about the order of existence that they formulate, meet and reinforce one another in ritual. The world as lived and the world as imagined, "fused under the agency of a single set of symbolic forms, turn out to be the same world."[29]

Another major function of ritual that must be considered here is to mark significant passages in human life. While participating in the ritual, people not only recognize, but also actually achieve transformation from one human state to another. Without these rituals, it may be difficult not only to recognize these transitions, but also to achieve them.

For example, humans traditionally have marked the transition from one stage of life to another by rites of passage. The transition from childhood to adulthood has been ritualized in many ways. Many Native American cultures, for example, performed rituals to recognize a girl's first menses. Ceremonies for boys might be quite formal, such as the public examination to which young Athenians submitted in order to exercise their rights as public citizens, or very intense and painful, such as submission to tooth extraction and scarification. Even in much of Europe and the United States during the eighteenth and early nineteenth centuries, for example, a boy's transition from short to long trousers marked the transition from childhood into puberty.

Contemporary rituals for passage into adulthood include a few religious ceremonies, such as bar and bat mitzvahs or confirmation, graduation, and activities such as voting, getting a driver's license, and moving out of the parents' home. However, without a ceremony to mark the transition, it is difficult for some contemporary youth to realize the passage into adulthood or, in fact, to become adults. This underscores the observation that rituals do more than indicate the significance of the moments and events that serve as their basis. They actually bring these moments and events into the present and make their truths effective.

It is because of their function to bring mythic truths to life that many rituals are characterized by repetition. For the most part, setting aside our inclination toward bigotry, human beings are in love with variety. We want that change of pace, that new idea, that different way of doing things. This is not our inclination, however, when it comes to ritual. When the officiant starts the words of a responsive reading, we need the pattern of the words to be effective, and that requires that the reading always be performed in the same way. That is why innovations to ritual are so problematic. More than mere resistance to change, we want our rituals to work.

There is another point to be made here. We have noted that the mythical worldview is more spiral than endless circle. In a real sense, anything which is repeated cannot be the same event which previously occurred, simply because it has taken place before. Considering repetitive patterns in poetry, Terry Eagleton points out that, "a word or image which is repeated does not mean the same as it did the first time, by virtue of the very fact that it is a repetition. No event occurs twice, precisely because it has occurred once already."[30]

Durkheim also stresses the importance of rituals to maintain our cultural and moral values. Rituals are experienced as effective and powerful because they remake individuals and communities morally.[31] In fact, rituals are as important to our moral lives as food is to our physical lives, because it is through rituals that groups affirm and maintain themselves. After participating in sacred rituals, individuals enter into their lives with greater courage and peace of mind, because they have been reinvigorated by a source of energy greater than themselves.[32]

Whether understood as setting the foundations of culture or cosmos, ritual practice must always be distinguished from mere routine. "Ritual is never simply or solely a matter of routine, habit or "the dead weight of tradition."[33]

All these definitions and explanations are of little use until they are applied to actual human experience. Before entering into the stories and exploring the mythic cycles themselves, it is worthwhile to note yet another unique human characteristic in relation to the cosmos. As far as we know, we are the only ones who are aware of the rest of it. Many literary accounts have paused to consider the wonder that humans experience as they gaze at the night sky. As creatures with intelligence, we ask what and how. As humans, we also want to know why. Gazing at the stars is not merely awe-inspiring; it is emotional. We feel our lives to be in some sort of relationship to the whole celestial array, and we want to reach out and somehow make contact with it. An old Leonard Cohen song lyric comes to mind: "We are so small between the stars, so large against the sky…."[34]

[chapter]

CREATION

There is a thing confusedly formed
Born before heaven and earth.
Silent and void
It stands alone and does not change,
Goes round and does not weary.
It is capable of being the mother of the world.
Dao De Jing

Among the questions that stir human curiosity, perhaps none is more compelling than the question of origin. As very small children, we ask, "Where did I come from?" Accompanying that question is the larger and even more fundamental question: "Why is it this way?" Lame accounts of storks and cabbage patches do little to soothe our earliest anxiety for understanding. The ancient creation stories, on the other hand, drew our ancestors into a profound sense of the meaning and nature of the world and of our place in it. "Etiological" myths are attempts to account for the origin of something such as a ritual practice or a natural phenomenon. On a grander scale, creation myths offer frameworks for understanding our ultimate origins.

Knowledge and theory about the *cosmos* belong to the intellectual category called "cosmology." The word cosmos is of Greek origin and means "ordered world," so cosmologies seek to understand, not only the nature of the world, but also the inner order to be found in the cosmos. The Greek philosopher and mathematician, Pythagoras, is said to have been the first to use the term to refer to the universe.

The term "cosmogony" more specifically refers to ideas about the *origin* of the cosmos, and symbolic narratives describing the earliest beginnings of the world and the place of humans in it are referred to as cosmogonic myths. While some earlier scholars thought of these stories as primitive science and analyzed them literally, creation myths are now understood as symbolic accounts serving as an orientation for people to the spiritual and natural world and to their place in it. Along the way, they have much to say about how people relate, or ought to relate, to one another.

In his classic study of creation stories, Charles Long notes that cosmogonic myths are the most fundamental of all myths. They are found in almost every culture and express in symbolic form "what is most essential to human life and society by relating it to a primordial act of foundation recorded in the myth."[1] Creation myths express humanity's "cosmic orientation" to time and space, to the rest of the living world, and to the powers that have established and continue to maintain our being in the world. This power or force is that which "centers and gives definiteness to the life of a human community. It is through a creative event that a new world, a definite order, is given to the stuff of history, the environment, and the psyche."[2]

Mythic creation accounts are as varied as the cultures from which they derive, and since one culture might well have several different creation stories, the variations are extremely complex. In a very real sense, every myth is unique and uniquely connected to its place of origin and the people who repeat it. However, scholars have noted that certain characteristics are true of virtually all creation myths. They are all narratives with a plot and characters. They all reveal something about the cultures from which they emerge, providing perspectives on deeply meaningful questions and the culture's self-identity. Though the specific themes of these stories vary, we can address certain similarities concerning the primordial state before creation, the creators, and the means of creation.

Resemblances among these stories, even from areas of the world far removed from one another, can be quite startling. Scholars have sought to group these stories in order to better understand them, and a number of methods now exist for categorizing them according to their central motifs.[3] While there are a number of common motifs to be found in creation stories, two great themes predominate: emergence and separation. Though they seem on the surface to contradict one another, these two themes are often both to be found in the same stories.

The theme of emergence in creation stories is the most obvious. This is intuitively familiar, and also confirmed by our scientific observations. When all the right circumstances come together, life emerges: out of the oceans, from our mothers' wombs, even out of a test tube. In the myths, the world often emerges out of a primordial ocean, a cosmic abyss, or the depths of the earth. Though less obvious, a second theme appears alongside the first. This is the theme of division, separation, and dismemberment. In this motif, creation is formed from the separated parts of what was once an undifferentiated whole.

Any classification of myths is to some extent deceptive. In fact, myths defy classification. Some myths contain both these themes, some emphasize one over the other, and others fit somewhere within one of the two, though other themes are likely to be present as well. Given this situation, it is not appropriate (nor, perhaps, very interesting) to force even a few creation myths into a common mold.

An additional relevant distinction involves the object of the creation. Some myths involve the creation of the entire universe, while others focus on the creation of human beings or of plant and animal life. These themes develop somewhat differently, depending on the scope and function of the creative acts in the myth.

―――――――――――――[chaos]―――――――――――――

Before we consider acts of creation, we must consider the primordial state that precedes them. This may at first seem rather odd. We are much more accustomed to the idea that nothing could possibly exist before creation. In the Genesis account, for example, the Hebrew term first used to refer to God's acts of creation, *bara,* is sometimes translated to mean creation out

of nothing [*creatio ex nihilo*].⁴ ⸺   owever, what most myths, Genesis included, describe. I⸺   os usually emerges or is formed
out of a pre-exi⸺   onment best described as chaos,
the abyss, ⸺   the primordial state before creation
includes ⸺   s darkness, wetness, formlessness, and
namele⸺   been represented as a monster: Leviathan,
the d⸺   e female monster of destruction, Behemoth; the
Bab⸺   r Vrtra, the first born of serpents in the Hindu Vedas.
⸺ ade attributes tremendous importance both to pre-cosmo-
g⸺ essness and to the cosmogony that alters and orders it. Such
⸺ e "myths to live by;" that is, they determine the pattern to be fol-
⸺ give meaning to human acts, and contribute to the identity of both
⸺ ommunity and the individual. Long holds that these myths express
⸺ ndamental power relationship in which the old must be destroyed in
⸺ der to make way for a new creation. The cosmos emerges over against
the chaotic void.⁵

[emergence]

Many myths depict creation as emerging out of the unfathomable abyss of chaos. In the Babylonian creation account, called the *Enuma Elish,* the first gods emerge from a primordial state in which the great sweet water ocean (Apsu, called the begetter) is commingled with the great salt-water ocean (Tiamat, the mother of all) in one body. It is a state described as prior to any constructions, when no gods were named and no destinies determined.

In the Genesis creation story, believed by many scholars to be related to the Babylonian account, this is *tehom*—the deep upon whose face is darkness—understood as formless waters over which moves the spirit or breath of God (Genesis 1.2). The Hebrew terms that are translated "without form and void" can also be translated as unseen and formless. This concept of the void parallels the Greek concept of Chaos, understood as a great gap or abyss at the beginning of the world.

In fact, there are hundreds of creation stories that involve emergence of creation out of water. This is not surprising. Water is an obvious symbol for the unformed, commingled state before creation, since water has no shape of its own. It is also an obvious symbol for the emergence of life. Not only are humans completely dependent upon water for life, but water (in the form of amniotic fluid) is also our first home. Our human birth is the fundamental paradigm for this emergence theme, as the mother's water breaks and new life emerges from her womb. The womb itself reflects the primordial condition, "the dark, hidden, chaotic, watery cavern from which life emerges."[6]

In some emergence myths, however, life comes not from the waters, but from the center of the earth. In these myths, the earth is viewed as a cosmic mother who brings forth the world. This motif is often associated with the creation of humans who emerge from the womb of the earth mother and pass from one world into another until they arrive on the surface of the earth. Long observes that by associating creation with the earth, this theme contains within itself "all of the potencies of life."[7] These myths depict the process by which humans progress from incompleteness to completeness, a conversion in which there is no immediate or violent transformation. "A certain type of harmony is present within the creative act."[8]

The creation that emerges may take many forms. In some myths, creation emerges out of chaos in the form of a cosmic egg. In others, deities emerge directly from the primordial realm as cosmic parents. However, creation cannot become complete until this initial union of creative forces is transformed. Therefore, these emergence themes are typically accompanied by motifs of separation or division as discussed below.

————————[separation and sacrifice]————————

We turn now to themes of separation, division, and dismemberment. Though at first this idea may appear to be antithetical to creation, we can glimpse the connection if we consider the development of human thought. We develop our understanding by learning the difference between one thing and another. We learn to distinguish colors, numbers, features of our world, and by forming these distinctions, we come to understand our surroundings. Language teaches us both similarity and difference. Children seek to discover how things work by taking them apart.

Certain myths depict this separation as a simple act of division, usually performed by a deity. In Genesis, God separates the waters above from the waters below and establishes a barrier between them so that the waters cannot flow back into one another. Another relatively benign separation motif is the separation of the primordial parents. In this imagery, the separations that take place do not constitute ruptures, and deep relationships between the separated parts may be maintained. These stories always commence with an initial union, typically the coming together of opposites such as earth and sky. Though their origins in the primal chaos express a totality or completeness, creation requires a dynamic separation so that a cosmic order and structure is formed "over against the rather indeterminate symbolism of the union of the divine couple." Typically, the children of the primordial parents, "motivated by a desire to acquire new life and knowledge," carry out this separation.[9] Similarly, this separation may be symbolized by the division of a cosmic egg, a concept strikingly similar to the division of cells.

In other mythic accounts, these divisions are symbolically represented through images of severing or cutting apart. Often but not always this theme is accompanied by symbolic accounts of sacrifice. Eliade stresses the ubiquity of the sacrificial theme in creation stories, observing that although it appears in various forms, the "mythic pattern remains the same: nothing can be created without immolation, without sacrifice."[10]

> The violent death is creative—in this sense, that the life which is sacrificed manifests itself in a more brilliant form upon another plane of existence.... A living "whole" bursts into fragments and disperses itself in myriads of animated forms. In other terms, here again we find the well-known cosmogonic pattern of the primordial "wholeness" broken into fragments by the act of Creation.[11]

This sacrifice is often made by a divine being who is murdered or commits an act of self-sacrifice. Philip Freund notes that in the mythic view, violent death is often perceived as a precondition for the emergence or re-emergence of life.[12]

Another related motif is the killing and dismemberment of a divine being or monster, from whose parts the creation is accomplished. Here we can note just a few examples. In a creation myth from Indo China, Pan Ku, the dwarf, transforms into a giant. When he dies, his body is magically transformed to create all the parts of the natural world. The Icelandic myth collection, the *Prose Edda,* tells of the hermaphrodite Rime-Giant called Ymir, who is slain by his sons and carried to the middle of the Yawning Void where they create the earth from parts of his body. The Indian Rg Veda tells of Purusa, both sacrificer and sacrificial offering, from whom all of the forms of humanity are made. In the great Mesopotamian epic, the Enuma Elish, the god Marduk conquers his primordial ancestress and creates the universe from the separated halves of her body. In dozens of myths related to the Polynesian islands, a young person, usually a woman, is murdered or sacrificed, dismembered, and buried, and all the edible plants grow from parts of her body. Some Native American myths reiterate this sacrificial theme to account for the creation of plants vital to the life of the people.

Joseph Campbell relates this sacrificial theme in cosmogony to sacrificial rituals performed by primal communities. Rather than representing gifts or bribes to the gods, these sacrifices are "fresh enactments, here and now, of the god's own sacrifice in the beginning, through which he, she, or it became incarnate in the world process."[13] These ritual acts "are functions and partial revelations of this immortal sacrifice."[14]

Certainly one of the most profound interpretations of this theme is that made by Mircea Eliade. In *The Myth of the Eternal Return,* Eliade notes the relationship between rituals performed by primal cultures at the beginning of any new building project and the reenactment of cosmogonic myth. Through sacrifice, a human construction is animated, endowed with a soul: "the prototype of the construction rite is the sacrifice that took place at the time of the foundation of the world."[15] The continuing endurance of human constructions, in fact their very reality, is founded upon repeating the divine act of sacrifice.

Another critical aspect of the sacrifice theme is the understanding that energy or power is released when the whole is divided. A scientific metaphor may prove useful here. The word "atom" literally means uncut or indivisible. However, when neutrons or other minute particles bombard the nucleus of the atom, the result is fission (literally a cleavage or splitting apart). The indivisible has been divided. When fission occurs, tremendous energy is released. Likewise, when the undifferentiated whole of chaos is split or shattered, the released energy is utilized (usually by a warrior deity) to create order from the parts. Charles Long notes that the sacrificial victim is always a residue of great power.

> The killing or sacrifice of these powerful beings effects a redistribution of power. Instead of the power residing in one being, it now flows into every part of the universe. It is made accessible to all beings. The parts of the sacrificed being become the stable and life-giving sources of the cosmos.[16]

There is, however, an inherent tension in the image of creation out of sacrifice. On the one hand, there is a bursting forth of restrained power moving out from the individual into the entire universe. On the other hand, there is a shattering of the whole, in order to produce a broken and fragmented creation. These myths face the reality of the life-and-death cycle. They not only perceive death as the necessary antecedent of creation, but also embrace the realization that new life sometimes emerges out of sudden and monstrous death. These images speak to the human experience of sacrificing for a greater good. If they free humanity from too much ego-involvement, they also speak to the fragmentation and dismemberment of the individual. These myths call us to psychic connection as we

recognize ourselves and our most intense longings and realizations reflected in their imagery.

For a deeper and more engaged exploration of origins, consideration
of overall themes can only take us so far. Finally, our understanding of
where we started and where we stand as human beings in a created world
is an emotional and spiritual matter. In order to explore this, we must engage the myths more intimately.

As indicated above, many mythic motifs are ubiquitous. Though the
details may shift and change, the overall ideas remain constant. Therefore,
we could explore many different myths to understand certain motifs revealed by these stories. Our practice here will be to focus in more detail on
one or two stories that clearly represent these ideas. Limiting the breadth
of our exploration can help us to engage more specifically with the depth
of meaning we find in these narratives.

For our consideration of creation motifs, we will utilize two stories
in particular. The first is the Babylonian creation story called the *Enuma
Elish,* briefly discussed above. The other is a Japanese creation account
found in one of the first books ever to be written in Japanese, the *Kojiki.*[17]
Details about the origins of these stories, their discovery, and the cultures
from which they emerge are readily available and would lend greater insight into the ways these stories interacted with human cultures. Here, as
previously discussed, we will focus on the content.

————————[male and female]————————

When we consider our own personal origins, one of the most fundamental
concerns is, of course, the sexual connection and the dynamic and often
problematic relationship between male and female at the heart of our con-
ception. It is interesting, therefore, that myths rarely overtly refer to the
sexual activity implicit in creation, although there are some remarkable
exceptions. The *relationship* between male and female, however, is at the
core of many creation stories.

As mentioned above, the *Enuma Elish* opens with a divine pairing, the
undifferentiated mingling of the salt water ocean (the male, called Apsu)
and the sweet water ocean (the female, called Tiamat). They begin by resting within one another in complete repose, but their very commingling
stirs procreation, and generations of gods begin to emerge from the depths.
As is often the case with progeny, they begin to raise a ruckus and disturb
their parents' rest. Apsu is all for destroying his children so that he can go
back to sleep, but Tiamat speaks in their favor. What follows is a wild tale

of political intrigue, betrayal, and power plays that, in its way, tells another story all too familiar to us.

Eventually, however, we find Tiamat enraged and preparing to do battle with one of her descendents, a warrior god called Marduk, chosen by the gods to defeat their primordial mother, because she has clearly had enough of them and is now plotting to destroy them. In a discussion between Marduk and his father, Anshar, regarding the pending battle, the gender issue is specifically addressed. Most translations put the following words into Marduk's mouth alone, although a more recent translation suggests that the following text is an exchange between Marduk and Anshar. The conversation opens with Marduk speaking:

> Father, don't stay so silent, open your lips,
> Let me go, and let me fulfil (sic) your heart's desire.
> …
> (Anshar replied)
> What kind of man has ordered you out (to) his war?
> My son, (don't you realize that) it is Tiamat, of womankind, who
> will advance against you with arms?
> (Marduk answered)
> Father, my creator, rejoice and be glad!
> You shall soon set your foot upon the neck of Tiamat![18]

Marduk's bragging would seem to indicate that he is not to be intimidated by any female. However, his preparations for battle belie his confidence. When he departs to face her, he is armed with a bow and arrow, a mace, lightning and flame, a net, seven winds, a flood weapon, and a storm chariot. In spite of his arrogance, he certainly appears to take the impending war with his primordial ancestress very seriously. We will return to this battle, but for the moment we must consider the gender question.

Tiamat's name is derived from the same root as *tehom;* she is the great Mother Monster of the depths. However, in the beginning, before any emergence or separation, she is the silently fecund mother of all. Her male consort, equally silent and still, is content merely to lay with her until the children wake him up, and he decides to kill the kids. Initially, Tiamat cries out on behalf of her offspring. Why, then, does she turn against them, and why do her descendants speak so contemptuously of womankind?

If the myths just portrayed the male/female relationship as a sleepy commingling, they would certainly represent only a tiny portion of the dynamic between woman and man. Once procreation has commenced, the action of the story intensifies, and conflict also commences. While father

Apsu tends to be merciless, Tiamat suggests kindness toward her trou-
blesome offspring. However, after they destroy her consort and conspire
against her, she transforms into the wrathful female, uttering curses and
crying out in fury.

The battle between Tiamat and Marduk is gratifyingly gory, but we
will skip over the details here and focus on the aftermath. After utterly
destroying Tiamat and all her armies, he turns to her body, "whom he
had ensnared:"

> The Lord trampled the lower part of Tiamat,
> With his unsparing mace smashed her skull,
> Severed the arteries of her blood,
> And made the North Wind carry it off as good news.
>
> ...
>
> The Lord rested and inspected her corpse.
> He divided the monstrous shape and created marvels (from it).
> He sliced her in half like a fish for drying:
> Half of her he put up to roof the sky,
> Drew a bolt across and made a guard hold it.
> Her waters he arranged so that they could not escape.[19]

Marduk goes on to perform other creative acts, including creating the
sky and teaching the stars how to shine.

On the surface, this story seems to symbolize the utter triumph of male
over female and also supports the association between the female and the
form or substance of the creation, leaving the action of creation to the
male. The cosmos is literally created from her body. However, there is one
small and very interesting detail that suggests another view. After Marduk
destroys Tiamat, he "ensnares" her—he ties her up. Since she is dead, this
hardly seems necessary.

In order to understand his actions, we must consider the incredible
resiliency of primordial chaos, especially as represented by the raging
female. For cultures that maintain ties to cyclical patterns of nature, the
powers of chaos are never completely eliminated. Eventually, "under their
persistent attack, time degenerates, confusion spreads, the world moves
to the edge of chaos."[20] These cultures typically performed annual rituals
in order to establish the purification and renewal necessary to overcome
the returning forces of chaos. In fact, the Babylonians ritually reenacted
this story every new year. It seems that the male may win out, but mother
chaos is never completely conquered.

In the Japanese creation story, though the plot and characters are very different, the dynamics between male and female, cosmos and chaos, are interestingly similar. As with the Babylonian creation story, the first heavenly deities emerge from chaos, described in the *Kojiki* as an ocean of oil and drift like a jellyfish. Unlike stories emerging from the Ancient Near East, however, this chaotic ocean is located on the Plain of High Heaven. Six generations of heavenly deities emerge, first as individuals and then as pairs. In the seventh generation, Izanagi (Male-Who-Invites) and Izanami (Female-Who-Invites) emerge and are instructed by their heavenly ancestors to "make, consolidate, and create this drifting land."[21] Taking with them a jeweled spear bestowed upon them by the gods of heaven, the pair stands together on the Floating Bridge of Heaven and dips the jeweled spear into the ocean of chaos. Together, they churn the oceans with the spear and then pull it from the brine. As they do so, congealed drops fall from the tip to form the first island of Japan, Onogoro.[22] Descending together onto the island, they erect a palace and a ceremonial pillar.

Some scholars have suggested that the creation story in the Kojiki is not truly a cosmogony, since it focuses on the creation of the islands and spiritual guardians of Japan rather than the whole world. Later Shinto scholars, however, suggest that the axis of the world passes through the very place of the celestial couple's first creation. It would seem that this island represents a microcosm through which the entire creation comes to be.

As with the Babylonian myth, creation begins with deities emerging from an ocean of chaos. However, the primordial creators are descendants rather than ancestors of the deities, and their creative acts are charged with sexual imagery. The jeweled spear with which they stir the ocean, lifting it up so that congealed drops fall from the tip, certainly appears to be a phallic image. If there is any doubt about the sexual symbolism of the spear, there can be no doubt about what follows.

The next part of the story is not as well-known as what precedes and follows it. When Chamberlain made his translation into English in 1917, he translated the parts he considered obscene into Latin, and most summaries leave this material out entirely. This omission is tragic, because it contains a crucial key to the male-female relationship and to the creation itself.

Izanagi and Izanami compare their bodies, revealing to one another that each has a particularly interesting body part. As they gaze upon one another, Izanagi initiates the conversation:

"How is your body formed?"

She replied saying:

"My body, formed though it be formed, has one place which is formed insufficiently."

Then Izanagi-nö-mikoto said:

"My body, formed though it be formed, has one place which is formed to excess."

After this discovery, Izanagi makes a suggestion: "I would like to take that place in my body which is formed to excess and insert it into that place in your body which is formed insufficiently, and [thus] give birth to the land. How would this be?" Izanami responds succinctly and affirmatively: "That will be good."[23]

Izanagi then suggests that they engage in a marriage ritual. Walking around the pillar in opposite directions, they meet face to face on the other side. When they meet, Izanami cries out in an expression of wonder and surprise: "How good a man." Izanagi replies with the same expression: "How good a woman."[24] There is, however, a problem. Izanagi notes that the ceremony has not been conducted properly, since the woman should not speak first. Their first two creations, a child and an island, are somehow deformed and are not to be counted as their children. When they report the problem to the heavenly deities, Izanagi's concerns are confirmed. The woman should not have been the first to speak. They must return and perform the ceremony correctly.

They follow this advice, and their creative acts now go well. However, a crucial interruption has occurred in their relationship. Prior to this moment, they have done everything as a couple. They stood side by side on the heavenly bridge, stirred the waters together, and united and celebrated their bodies together. Up to this point in the story, their names, their actions, and their words have been exactly and specifically parallel. With the proclamation that the woman should not speak first, the first element of hierarchy comes between them, a breach that will eventually separate them completely.

After having given birth to numerous offspring, including various islands and the gods of winds, trees, mountains, and plains, Izanami gives birth to the fire deity who unintentionally burns her genitals so that she falls ill and dies. Izanagi grieves for her and buries her, but he cannot continue creation without her and eventually decides to seek her in the underworld. Finding her, he begs her to return so that they can complete the creation together. She is moved by his plea but indicates that since she has eaten in the land of the dead, she must seek permission to depart. Before she leaves, she instructs him very firmly not to look at her. Her absence is lengthy, however, and Izanagi grows impatient. He lights a fire from one of the end-teeth in his comb and rushes into the adjoining chamber. There he finds Izanami in an advanced state of decay, with maggots "squirming and roaring" in her corpse. From various parts of her body, thunder deities are emerging. Izanagi is terrified and flees. Izanami, angry and offended, then pursues him, accompanied by numerous thunder-deities and warriors.

When Izanagi finally emerges from the passage to the underworld, just ahead of his angry spouse, he rolls a huge boulder over the opening to block the passage. Once again, the celestial couple faces one another, this time from opposite sides of the stone. Izanami again speaks first, threatening to bring death to the populace as a result of his actions. Izanagi replies, indicating that he will cause fifteen hundred births for every thousand beings that Izanami destroys. Interestingly, in this final conversation between them they still refer to one another as "beloved."

From this point on, Izanami is queen of the underworld. Eventually, Izanagi ascends to the heavens. Now the first creators are totally and completed separated. He has ascended all the way up into the heavens. She has descended all the way down into the underworld. There is a boulder between them. But once, in the beginning, they stood side by side on the heavenly bridge.

This creation story reiterates the themes of emergence and separation. It also confirms that in the style of such powerful myths, this cosmogony brings together oppositions: death as well as life, decay as well as growth, separation as well as union. The primordial male-female relationship begins in complete harmony and gradually disintegrates as greater and greater hierarchy intervenes.

These creation stories and others explore the interaction between emergence and separation themes as they reveal the dynamics of chaos and cosmos, male and female. However, there are a number of additional motifs revealed here. Though they appear not only in cosmogonic myths, but in other narratives as well, these creation stories provide us with an entry to unraveling them.

[the face-to-face encounter]

In the realm of myth, opposing forces do not merely come into contact with one another. They confront one another face-to-face. There are so many illustrations of this encounter that we have come to expect it. As the battle rages, whether in written narratives or films, we wait for the moment when the two antagonists, representing opposite sides, will meet face-to-face and do battle. This is Peter Pan and Captain Hook, Luke Sky-walker and Darth Vader, St. George and the dragon. This is also Marduk and Tiamat on the battlefield, Izanagi and Izanami on opposite sides of the boulder. All the supporting armies on either side fade into the background, and the opponents confront one another in a cosmic face off.

Much also is revealed by the failure to face one's enemy. Before Marduk comes upon the scene, a couple of Tiamat's descendants, Ea and Anu, are charged by their father with going to speak with her in an attempt to calm her down. However, these attempts fail because each one, at the critical moment, is afraid to face her.

> "My father, Tiamat's actions were too much for me.
> …
> Her strength is mighty, she is completely terrifying.
> …
> I feared her shout, and I turned back.
> But father, you must not relax, you must send someone else to her.
> However strong a woman's strength, it is not equal to a man's."

Though these deities also utter disparaging remarks about her gender, her rage clearly terrifies them. In the earliest moments of the chaos cosmos encounter, the powers of life and death enter into a direct and immediate relationship. Failure to "face up" to this encounter leads to defeat.

Of course, face-to-face encounters in myth are not necessarily battles. When Izanami and Izanagi first gaze upon one another and observe their sexual differences, they are not antagonized but delighted. The point is that they do not turn away. They are willing to explore their differences and to utilize their opposing energies in order to bring about a new creation.

These myths underscore an essential realization. We fear most what we cannot face, and we cannot really learn about the "other," whoever or whatever it may be, without a genuine encounter. The myths call us to become more aware of what happens when we turn away. In contemporary culture, technology provides us with many means to communicate, but also it provides us with many ways to avoid a face-to-face encounter. Wars are fought with targets in the crosshairs, and humans kill one another without ever seeing their faces. We spend so much time gazing at screens, typing and texting without ever seeing the faces of those with whom we seek to make contact. These ancient stories remind us that without gazing into the face of the unknown, we can never understand it.

————————————{ naming }————————————

In the ancient world, a name was much more than a label, and naming was thought to be an extremely powerful act. Invoking or calling a spirit or deity by name might summon its power. Likewise, a demon could not be expelled unless it was first forced to give up its name. In some cases, the power lay in the name itself, while other narratives stressed the power to bestow names upon others.

In ancient Egypt, all these powers came together. Names were given immediately at birth, since they were considered to be an important component of the soul, and continuing existence depended upon preservation of one's name. The ability to create and destroy was associated with knowledge of true names.

Some Egyptian creation accounts record that the Egyptian god Re (also Ra), god of the sun, brought all forms of life into existence by speaking their secret names. Re's daughter, Isis, wished to learn Re's own secret name, so that she and her son, Horus, could have equal power. As Re crossed from horizon to horizon, he grew old, and his spittle fell upon the earth. Isis mixed his heavenly drool with earth to form a sacred serpent, which she then placed directly in Re's path. The great god was bitten and immediately overcome by the serpent's poison. Crying out in pain, Re called all his heavenly children to his aid. Among them was Isis who told Re to reveal his secret name to her so that he could be healed by its power. After some attempts at evasion, Re finally consented to have his name pass from him into Isis, although he required that she and her son keep it secret from others. Once she had taken his secret name, Isis drove the poison from him, but she now also had his power.

In the mythic realm, to give something or someone a name or to call others by name is always to assert a significant relationship. In many traditions, including the Abrahamic faiths, the names of God are sacred and function at a much deeper level than mere identification. In some cases, however, naming indicates authority of the namer over the named. At various points in Hebrew scripture, God bestows a new name upon someone (like Abraham) in order to indicate a new relationship. The power to name is given to the man in Genesis 2 and will be discussed at greater length below.

————————————{ the myth of the forbidden thing }————————————

Another motif is so familiar to us that we often fail to realize how deeply rooted it is in our perceptions and expectations. Scholars who analyze familiar motifs in folktales and myths typically refer to this motif as "the forbidden chamber." Two dynamics are always present in these stories. First, something is directly and specifically forbidden. Though the name derives from the prohibition against entering a particular room, there are numerous examples of prohibited acts and objects. Some entity, often a deity, specifically forbids a particular act such as opening a door or a box, eating a particular fruit, or, as in the case of Izanagi's adventures in the underworld, looking upon a particular sight. The second dynamic always present in this motif is that whatever is forbidden will at some point be done. The fruit will be eaten, the box will be opened, what was hidden will be revealed. And the consequences will always be dire. These prohibitions usually carry with them not only the threat of punishment, however, but also a hidden promise of revealed secrets or greater knowledge.

Some scholars have interpreted these images as warnings against female curiosity and disobedience, referring to examples such as Eve and Pandora. However, as in the Japanese story, there are also numerous accounts of males entering into whatever area or action has been specifically forbidden. Orpheus, for example, cannot help looking back to see if his beloved Eurydice is following him out of the underworld, and this glance costs him everything.

Like the face-to-face encounter, this motif reveals more than what is in the box or behind the door. What is at stake here is nothing less than some of the most fundamental aspects of human nature. These stories constantly remind us that we are the ones who invariably defy prohibitions and poke our noses into whatever we don't understand, no matter what the risk. From childhood on, an instruction to stay out of the closet causes that closet to become endlessly fascinating. Being told that something is none of our business causes us to pursue what might not otherwise be so intriguing. As humans, we are the ones who want to know, and the myths remind us that this knowledge comes with a price.

————————[putting it all together]————————

The creation myth shared, in one version or another, by the Abrahamic faiths was first set out at the beginning of the first book of Torah in the Hebrew Bible, known to Christians as the book of Genesis in the Old Testament. Having considered various themes and motifs of creation stories, an in-depth exploration of this creation story vividly illustrates the ways in which cosmogonies reveal ultimate truths in symbolic language. There are so many subtle facets of this narrative that literally thousands of texts have been written to analyze every minute facet. It would be quite impossible to consider them all here, but the specific themes previously discussed all make their appearance in one form or another.

It might be worthwhile here to repeat that sacred stories are mythic in that their truths are too complex and multifaceted to be told in literal discursive language. Unlike fantasies or folktales, myths communicate humanity's most profound search for truth and understanding. The position taken here is not so much that Genesis is not literally true, but that a literal interpretation of this cosmogony shortchanges it. There is more truth here than could ever be revealed by a mere "factual" account.

As has already been discussed, Genesis opens with the spirit of God gliding over the depths of *tehom*. Creation begins with light, emerging from the call or command of God. Since God doesn't call the sun and the moon into being until the fourth day, questions present themselves: What is God's light? What is a day to God? Even the ancient ones seemed to have had an understanding that the light of God preceded mortal measurements of time.

After the emergence of light, the theme of creation by division does not take long to emerge. As with any aspect of scripture, there is debate about the nature of the dome or firmament that God set between the waters above and the waters below. What is clear is that God intended to separate them. A common understanding of the ancient worldview is that the upper world was separated from the nether world by the vast dome of the heavens, made of some solid substance such as metal or congealed water vapor, over which the sun, moon and stars made their passage. Others suggest that this vast dome was supported by pillars of earth. Waters without separation will merge. Remembering that the terms tehom and Tiamat are related, this act of separation brings to mind Marduk's posting of guards to keep the waters of chaos from escaping.

Long before humans come into the picture, Genesis reveals much about the nature of the universe. One aspect of God's creation very rarely takes center stage when analyzing Genesis. In the beginning, God created monsters, and more specifically, sea-monsters. After generally mentioning creatures that fly, swim and swarm, the story specifically narrates that God creates *tanniyn*. This term appears 28 times in the Bible and is most often translated as dragon, although it appears to be a fairly general term and is also translated as sea or river monster or whale. Whatever theological interpretations may follow, the story itself is quite specific that sea-monsters and serpents are God's creations. In the psalms, God both fights and plays with these monsters. Chaotic elements are understood here, as in other cosmogonies, as a significant aspect of divine creative acts.

The male/female dynamic in Genesis is certainly one of the most ana-lyzed (perhaps over-analyzed) aspects of scripture. Most scholars agree that there are two different creation narratives in Genesis 1-3, with two different descriptions of the creation of man and woman. The first appears at Genesis 1:26-27 and relates the simultaneous creation of the first man and the first woman, both created in the image of God. In the second story at Genesis 2:21-22, the first living thing created by God is *ad'ham* (best translated as humankind), made from *ad'hama* (dust or earth), and Eve, the last created being, is specifically created to be a worthy companion or helper to *ad'ham.*

What is the nature of the male/female relationship here? That may be a bit like asking what God intended the human role to be in the world. A case can be made that humans were created to be the owners of the garden (to have dominion as in Genesis 1: 28) and also that we were put here to be the gardeners (Genesis 2:15, "to till the land and keep it").

Genesis 1 seems clearly to indicate that men and women were cre-ated simultaneously in the image of God. The term in Genesis 2 that is translated "helper" never appears elsewhere in the Bible as a term for an inferior. However, the curses at Genesis 3 would indicate that, at least after the "fall," the man was to rule over the woman. One Rabbinic approach to reconciling the texts suggests that God first created a woman (whom they called Lilith) together with the man and later created Eve out of the man, because Lilith, being equal to the man, did not know her place and refused to lie beneath him. Lilith was then expelled from the garden and flew away.

Naming is another important motif in Genesis. There is no specific mention of God naming *ad'ham* (hence, translating Adam as a proper name in the garden of Eden story may well be an error), but the task of naming every other creature is specifically bestowed upon the man. As indicated above, this power of naming may give the man authority over the other creatures. Interestingly, however, he does not name his new wife until just before he is driven out of the garden. It is worth noting that the name he gives her means "mother of all living."

There is an interesting discrepancy here, since Eve, being the last cre-ation, had no role in creating any of the other living creatures. Whose mother is she? Since ancient goddesses were frequently known by similar titles (see, for example, the Tiamat story above), Eve's name may reveal a trace of earlier goddess traditions. Perhaps the ancient authors were in-tentionally replacing these traditions with one in which human creative power trumps the divine mother. Perhaps, rather than representing literal childbearing, her motherhood refers to her nature as the primordial female.

It is also interesting to note that the man does not name her until after they are cursed. Perhaps his understanding of her nature comes from the knowledge acquired from the forbidden fruit. Perhaps he does not have the authority to name her until Genesis 3:16 curses her with his ruling power.

What about the face-to-face encounter? In the anthropomorphic language of Genesis 2 and 3, God directly confronts the man and the woman with their disobedience. In this narrative, there is an interesting turning away. The man not only blames the woman for his forbidden act but also blames God: "The woman *whom you gave to be with me,* she gave me fruit from the tree, and I ate" (emphasis mine). The woman also passes the buck, blaming the serpent for tempting her.

Among the motifs discussed above, perhaps the most obvious is the myth of the "forbidden thing." In Genesis 1, God does not forbid eating any of the fruit in the garden. However, in Genesis 2 and 3, the forbidden fruit from the tree of knowledge of good and evil has a central place in the story.

What really tempts the woman? The text mentions that the fruit is beautiful and appears to be tasty, but it also specifically states that the woman desired it for the wisdom that it would bring. She wanted to know. When the man and woman eat the fruit, their eyes are open. No longer innocent, they can no longer remain in the garden but must go off to be human. God curses them, as well as the serpent, with their own nature. The serpent must crawl on its belly and eat dust, the man must work on the land and till the soil by the sweat of his brow, and the woman must suffer the pains of childbirth. This is certainly not paradise, but there is no terrible torture or brutality here. Go then, says God, and be human. Apparently, God did not need to question the serpent.

———————{ first and last }———————

Since scholars became aware of paradigm shifts, we have known that our worldviews profoundly affect the ways that we perceive reality, and that our ways of understanding the world change as our symbol systems change. It is extraordinary, then, to note that the images in these very old stories are echoed in some of the most current imagery of contemporary physics.

In fact, the earliest stories of creation can be eerily similar to the most recent cosmological descriptions. In the beginning, there was light. Einstein found this light in an elementary particle called the photon, a quantum of electromagnetic energy thought to be a discrete particle having zero mass, no electric charge, and an indefinitely long lifetime. Earlier we considered the question of God's light in Genesis. Einstein has provided us with an answer that suggests the existence of cosmic light eons before the arrival of the sun and the moon.

Assuming that there is only one universe (though some theories suggest otherwise), most contemporary physicists now believe that about 80% of the matter in the universe consists of dark matter. Without getting into the scientific complexities, scientists have hypothesized the existence of dark matter to account for observed discrepancies that arise when various methods are used to measure the universe. Although this dark matter is inferred to exist based on gravitational effects on visible matter and background radiation, it has thus far remained undetectable. Though the existence of dark matter is widely accepted in the scientific community, we have no direct evidence of its existence and no understanding of its nature. The most advanced scientific techniques have brought us to an awareness that the majority of the universe is dark and unknowable—tehom.

Among the many interesting observations based on the idea of the Big Bang, this theory suggests that, rather than being eternal, the universe had a beginning. Additionally, the matter and energy formed from this initial event can neither be created nor destroyed, although it can revert to other forms. Energy is matter without tangible form; matter is energy in tangible form. All of the matter and energy that exist in the universe have existed since their initial creation.

Ancient cosmogonies describe this initial act in myriad ways, but they all concur that a cosmic event occurs, establishing the basis for everything that follows. Returning to the Babylonian epic, Marduk destroys Tiamat by filling her with air, so that her belly is distended, and then piercing her with a spear. Anyone that has ever popped a balloon with a pin will recognize in this description a very early symbolic reflection of the big bang.

Many other symbolic descriptions in ancient cosmogonies are reflected in contemporary science. The division of the cosmic egg into halves that then subdivide is basic embryology. That life emerged from the sea, and that creatures of the sea and air preceded creatures of the land, is an elementary biological concept. Even the basic struggle between order and chaos is repeated endlessly in everything from species selection to the phenomenally complex and carefully ordered human immune system.

Though some theories have been offered to account for these paradigmatic similarities, this harmony between ancient views and contemporary descriptions is not so strange. We do not need to resort to aliens with knowledge of the future or prophets with divine foreknowledge. Our knowledge of the cosmos has developed along with human evolution, but there is still much more mystery than certainty. As beings that wish to know about our world, we create symbolic structures to guide our explorations. Whether these are ancient narratives or scientific descriptions, they are always only partial. We stand where our ancient ancestors stood, gazing up at the night sky, and we do what we can with it.

[chapter]

HEROES AND GODS

We need the tonic of wildness… At the same time that we are earnest
to explore and learn all things, we require that all things be mysterious
and unexplorable, that land and sea be indefinitely wild, unsurveyed and
unfathomed by us because unfathomable.

H.D. Thoreau

We turn now to more familiar territory. If asked what images come to mind when thinking about myths, perhaps most people would refer either to the sexual and political exploits of Greek and Roman deities, or to the heroic journeys of such adventurers as Ulysses, Odysseus, and Jason. Here, too, however, we discover powerful truths revealed within the symbolic structure of the stories. The characteristics and exploits of gods and heroes carry our imaginations to realms beyond the ordinary, and suggest possibilities that could not otherwise be imagined.

Temporarily setting aside the vast and complex realm of the divine in mythology, we first will consider one of the most significant and powerful aspects of the mythic world view: the hero's journey. If creation stories were Mircea Eliade's idea of the most foundational myths, for Joseph Campbell all myths derive from what he termed the "monomyth." Campbell borrowed this term from James Joyce's *Finnegan's Wake* to refer to a formula he believed to be the basis for the entire mythic worldview: The hero departs from the everyday world and enters a region of supernatural wonder. After encountering fabulous forces and undertaking tremendous challenges, the hero returns from this mysterious adventure with new abilities, including the capacity to benefit others.[1]

As already mentioned, Campbell and most of the scholars who have followed him focused predominantly on male figures and interpreted the heroic journey along masculine lines. For Campbell, all the great mythologies were from the male point of view, and women figured into the stories as those who endured and waited for the return of the hero.[2] This perspective has been much critiqued, and some scholars have attempted to explore this "monomyth" from a female point of view, suggesting that women's journeys may differ from the male paradigm.[3]

Though Campbell's account of this mythic paradigm has influenced my own interpretation, it is my view that the hero's journey is a human experience, not merely a masculine one. Certainly, men and women may experience the stages of this journey differently, although I believe that attempts to describe these differences likely take us into very murky waters. However, it is my position that the basic stages of this motif, as described below, apply to both genders. I have illustrated this position with some female examples of the hero's journey. However, I find the term "heroine" to be awkward and misleading, so I have avoided using it here.

Like the overall dynamic of the mythic worldview, the hero's journey is cyclical in nature, departing from, and returning to the starting place. Unlike some epics and legends, however, these journeys are not so much about the destination or the goal, but about the inner development and realizations achieved by the heroes. Most fundamentally, heroic discoveries are always about ourselves. As Campbell describes it, "The passage of the mythological hero may be overground, incidentally; fundamentally it is inward—into depths where obscure resistances are overcome, and long lost, forgotten powers are revivified, to be made available for the transfiguration of the world."[4] These journeys are not only about attainment, but also about discovering again what has been in the heart of the hero the entire time. "From this point of view the hero is symbolical of that divine creative and redemptive image which is hidden within us all, only waiting to be known and rendered into life."[5]

————————[the call]————————

Though this description of the hero's journey will vary from Campbell's model, we begin where he begins, with the "call." As humans, we have a tendency to seek comfort and security. When we feel safe and comfortable, a kind of torpor sets in, and we hesitate to take any action that might put this state at risk. Therefore, an adventure typically requires some sort of crisis that precipitates the hero away from the comforts of hearth and home and into the unknown. This crisis may be a sudden personal catastrophe, such as a death in the family or some form of danger that threatens. It also may take much less dramatic form, such as a strong feeling of restlessness or longing that overpowers the desire to remain safe and secure. The crisis may occur throughout the community. Perhaps an invading army threatens or the community has fallen on hard times and cannot survive unless a hero undertakes a quest to resolve the crisis. In the great world-historical or apocalyptic myths, as Campbell points out, the entire physical and spiritual life of the planet may be on the verge of falling into ruin.[6]

Whatever the precipitating factors might be, this call becomes a kind of awakening. The comfortable patterns of the past no longer fit, and one must cross the threshold into a new world. The mythic realm into which the hero enters is a land of both treasure and danger, "but it is always a place of strangely fluid and polymorphous beings, unimaginable torments, superhuman deeds, and impossible delight."[7] Whether the hero undertakes the journey intentionally, is captured and dragged to it, or merely blunders into it by mistake, the call to adventure always represents the transfer of the hero's spiritual center of gravity from the security of society to the realms of the unknown.[8] This boundary crossing into a new way of being is the first of many passages.

─────────────────────────────────[companions]───────────────────────────────

Though almost all heroes must sometimes travel alone, such an adventure also typically involves many others. These may range from faithful companions to dangerous enemies, from tempters who lure the hero away from the goal to wise strangers who provide just what is needed to go forward.

When the journey begins in the company of others, these companions may represent many different dynamics. One frequent fellow traveler is the "faithful sidekick." This being is almost always of the same gender as the hero and undertakes the adventure specifically to be of service or support. Though sidekicks do not commence the journey with their own quests in mind, they may well discover their own goals and part company with the hero, at least for a time. These faithful followers often represent a form of knowledge or wisdom that supports the hero, although this wisdom is often ignored. These companions may take the form of a wise fool, such as Don Quixote's squire, Sancho, or Frodo's Sam. They may also represent a sort of clear-eyed practicality, such as Tonto provides for the Lone Ranger.

On the other hand, there are many companions whose function is to impede the progress of the hero. These may be traitors in disguise with a secret mission of sabotage. They may be lazy or careless, causing delays and accidentally endangering others. An interesting variation on this theme is the companion who starts out as an impediment and undergoes his or her own transformation, becoming a trusted and useful friend.

No matter how mysterious and fanciful the hero's adventures might be, we are drawn to these stories in part because they are familiar. We recognize ourselves in the challenges, the failures and triumphs of the hero. Our own personal journeys begin when we depart from the security of home and family. This may be a symbolic departure, such as acquiring a driver's license. It may be more literal, such as going away to college or moving into one's own apartment. Of course, it also may begin with a crisis, when there is no safety or security at home or one's personal experience becomes so dire that there are few alternatives except to undertake an adventure.

Our own companions, too, vary in their ability to support and to distract. Many of us know the experience of growing apart from the friends of our youth and inviting new and different people into our lives. Most of us also know the experiences of being supported at times of great need and being betrayed by those we thought we could trust.

There are some specific symbolic meetings on the hero's journey that require particular consideration. Primary among these is the "old wise one," an archetypal being who represents a unique encounter with the hero.

This meeting often occurs early in the journey, providing the hero with an opportunity to acquire critical protection or wisdom. Often, the wise one appears at a crossroads. Since this crossroads encounter is such a critical aspect of the hero's journey, it is worthwhile to consider it more closely.

———————[the caterpillar's question]———————

A crossroads in a hero's journey represents any point of critical choice. It literally may be a place where roads come together, either at an intersection or a fork in the road. It also may be expressed as a choice between doors or gates or even a choice between objects or actions. The defining feature is that the hero can only choose one of the alternatives. Once the choice is made, and the hero goes forward, it may be difficult or impossible to return to the site and choose differently.

Here at the crossroads, we often find the old wise one, usually in disguise and often appearing to be in need of help. The hero's decisions here are critical. If the opportunity to benefit from the wisdom of this stranger is missed, the future journey will be much more difficult. If, however, the hero recognizes the possibilities of this encounter and offers the needed help, the old, wise one will offer critical advice and assistance, though its usefulness may not be apparent at the time. Often, the wise one also bestows some sort of charm or gift upon the hero, though here again this gift may appear to have little or no value. It is up to the hero to recognize its potential and care for the gift until its powers are made known.

These crossroads meetings are among the most significant aspects of the hero's journey. Here, certain qualities and characteristics of the traveler are revealed, often at an early stage of the adventure. When Alice pauses in front of the caterpillar to inquire as to the appropriate direction to take, the caterpillar does not provide her with a map or suggest a route. Rather, he asks the most critical question one can ask at any crossroads: "Who are you?" Throughout the hero's adventures, at every obstacle and opportunity, that is the critical question the hero must face. The answer to the riddle of choice always lies in the heart of the one who must choose.

Another character test comes about when the hero meets a gatekeeper. Heroes' journeys are often constructed as a series of steps or stages, and entry to another level may depend on getting through some sort of passage or gate. Here, the gatekeeper also represents a test of character. Riddles the hero must solve or tasks the hero must perform are more than mere challenges. Overcoming the obstacle presented by the gatekeeper provides the hero with necessary skills or character traits to move forward. Proper interaction with the gatekeeper is critical to a successful journey, and sometimes wisdom acquired through a prior meeting with the old wise one can be useful in accomplishing this passage. Once the hero has passed the critical tests, gatekeepers may also become guides, teachers, or conductors of souls from one region to another.

As the hero passes from one zone of experience into another, each passage leads deeper into the unknown. In myths all over the world, from the Greeks to the Welsh to the pre-Columbians of the Bahamas, the underworld is guarded by monstrous gatekeepers. Though the guardians at the boundaries may be dangerous, and such passages are risky, the danger can be overcome by proceeding with competence and courage. Gatekeepers may protect places of great wealth or power to prevent the uninitiated from entering, but they may also guard the threshold to keep those who have already crossed over from escaping.[9]

————————[obstacles and encounters]————————

One key difference between a hero's journey and other traveler's tales is that a hero faces increasingly difficult obstacles that must be overcome. These may take the form of tasks that must be performed, such as the twelve labors of Hercules or Jason's quest for the Golden Fleece. They may also arise as impediments to achieving a certain goal. When Frodo sets out to destroy the One Ring in Tolkien's classic *Lord of the Rings,* all the forces of evil arise to prevent him from succeeding, including the darkness in the ring itself. Facing these obstacles often involves encounters with supernatural power, sometimes in the form of beings representing the hero's most significant internal struggles.

One such archetypal encounter a hero might face is confrontation with a shadow figure. We have discussed the symbolic significance of the face-to-face encounter in myth. Often, this face off involves a direct confrontation with the hero's own dark opposite. The god Janus is depicted with two heads facing in opposite directions, sometimes representing dualities or opposites. The term Janus-faced may be used to describe one who feels one way and acts in another. In mythical confrontations, heroes often face the dark side of their own nature. In his fabulously successful *Star Wars* franchise, George Lucas borrowed very consciously from Campbell's model of the hero's journey. Luke Skywalker's battle with Darth Vader is the epitome of the face-to-face encounter, and it is critical that Luke's enemy is related to him. While he is fighting the Dark Force, Luke must battle that same force within himself.

Not all challenging encounters are with obvious villains. In fact, among the most dangerous encounters a hero must face is with those who represent temptation. Many great religious figures, including Buddha and Jesus, faced and overcame temptation. Both Odysseus and Jason faced Sirens whose beautiful songs drew sailors toward them until they crashed on the rocks. Sometimes the temptation comes, not from an outside source, but from within, as the hero settles for comfort, love, or peace rather than continuing the journey. Shakespeare's characters often were distracted or put to sleep with magic flowers (probably the wild pansy, sometimes called "heart's ease"), and a field of poppies overcame Dorothy and friends. Though heroes may discover and be strengthened by love along the way, they may also be distracted or sidetracked by sexual desire, wealth, or power.

One of the greatest hero's-journey epics is that of Gilgamesh, a legendary Sumerian king, who sets out to obtain immortality. In a cave beside the sea that surrounds the world, he encounters a veiled woman who is actually a manifestation of the goddess Ishtar. She encourages him not to pursue his quest, but to be content with the mortal joys of life:

> Gilgamesh, why dost thou run about this way?
> The life that thou art seeking, thou wilt never find.
> When the gods created man,
> they put death upon mankind,
> and held life in their own hands.
> Fill thy belly, Gilgamesh;
> day and night enjoy thyself;
> prepare each day some pleasant occasion. ...[10]

When Gilgamesh resists this temptation and determines to go forward, the concealed goddess permits him passage and warns him of the dangers ahead.

Again, it is worth noting that these stories have such significance to us because we recognize them. We know all too well what it means to come up against a choice we do not know how to make or an obstacle that seems too great to overcome. The individuals who repel us because they remind us of suppressed aspects of ourselves are as familiar as the gatekeepers who hold some promise, such as a diploma or a promotion, just out of reach until we solve their riddles. We also are, of course, very familiar with temptations that catch us up in procrastination and lethargy.

the ultimate obstacle

There are heroes who slay all the dragons, accomplish all the mighty feats, win all the battles, and return home in triumph. These are not, however, the heroes of the mythic journey. Mythic symbolism takes us deeper into inner realms, and at the moment of the ultimate test, true heroes often fail. They come upon the door that cannot be opened, the beast that cannot be slain, or the problem that cannot be solved. They fall off cliffs, collapse inert in the snow, and even get devoured. They die.

In his study of the relationship between archaic and contemporary myths and rituals, Eliade observes the significance of ritual death as part of primal initiation rites. In these traditions, he takes the position that symbolic death is always the ground for regeneration.[11] In the realm of the mythic, "one had to die to something to be able to be reborn."[12] This is what the hero's journey is really all about. One cannot accomplish the journey from birth to resurrection without those messy moments in between.[13] The mythic cycle reminds us that death and decay are as critical to transformation as are birth and growth. In fact, the enormous release of energy we find in the realm of chaos is absolutely critical for new life to emerge. In many myths, this is the beginning of a journey within the journey—the descent into the underworld and, if the hero stays the course, the return.

Much scholarship and speculation concentrates on the journey to the underworld, and the following chapter will focus entirely on this topic. Here, we will pause briefly to note another mythic puzzle. Within the answer to this puzzle lies another significant aspect of the hero's journey symbolism. The puzzle is this: From culture to culture, from story to story, the underworld is always described as the land of no return. In fact, this is the most consistent characteristic of the underworld. The puzzle then becomes obvious. Heroes' journeys would come to nothing if heroes descended into the underworld and just stayed there. Why are there so many stories about emerging or returning from the underworld? How is this possible? Myths do not cheat or beat around the bush. Hell is not just a little bit hell. You cannot get out. If you want to emerge from the underworld, the one who descended cannot be the one who returns. Now the *solution* becomes obvious. The underworld descent and return is, by definition, transformative. At the heart of the netherworld, the old self dies, and a new self emerges. The hero may, as Campbell notes, be "born back into the world from which he came," but this new self is not the same as the one who descended. This surrender of the ego (or death of the ego-self) is the essential factor for the ascent into new life out of the "land of no return."[14]

———————————{ transformation }———————————

The cycle of birth, life, death, transformation, and rebirth is at the core of mythic symbolism, and each hero's journey reflects this pattern to some extent. For ancient cultures, this cycle was extremely familiar. As noted above, the archaic worldview required that every new creation be preceded by a return to chaos; the old must be annihilated so that the new could emerge. Myths depicting this aspect of the hero's journey have an initiatory structure, and ancient initiatory rituals reflected this pattern of descent, death, transformation, and restoration. Initiatory death was symbolized in a variety of ways, including a symbolic return to the womb or a perilous journey into the center of the earth or the mouth of a monster. This entry into the netherworld prepared the initiate for "birth to a higher mode of being."[15] Although this dark world began by representing the realm after death, it came to symbolize a place where secret knowledge could be attained, mortality cast aside, and transcendence attained.[16]

Primal shamanic rituals also specifically depicted this cycle. Here, the shaman must die and be reborn so that the sick individual (and the entire community) can be healed. Anthropologist Joan Halifax vividly describes this journey as experienced by the Siberian Yakuts:

> The ... shaman enters the gloomiest of forests and traverses the highest of mountains. Everywhere are the bones of shamans and their mounts who have died while voyaging in these forsaken wastelands. At last, the shaman comes upon a hole in the earth and begins the journey in the Underworld Realm. In the Land of the Dead, spirits of disease haunt the shaman, and the souls of transgressors reveal their terrifying fate with violent gestures. The shaman then confronts the Lord of the Underworld, who howls and bellows like a maddened bull.[17]

Halifax notes, "The encounter with death and dying and the subsequent experience of rebirth and illumination are the authentic initiation for the shaman."[18] These healers must learn the art of dying in order to gain the knowledge necessary for healing particular illnesses. "The territory of disease has been revealed to them, and they can now guide the suffering across the terrain of sickness and even death."[19]

During this underworld journey, the shaman may be subjected to ritual dismemberment performed by spirits, during which the old self may be cleansed or reconstructed. Eliade describes a shamanic account of a great Bird-of-Prey Mother with an iron beak, hooked claws, and a long tail. This spirit bird takes the soul of the shaman, carries it to the underworld, and leaves it there to ripen on the branch of a pine tree. When it has ripened to maturity, the bird returns the body to earth, cuts it into pieces, and distributes it among the evil spirits of disease and death, giving the shaman the ability to cure corresponding diseases. Afterward, the Bird-Mother restores the bones to their proper places, and the shaman wakes from trance with the necessary healing knowledge and power.[20]

This pattern also is reflected in the rituals of the mystery cults that emerged in the Greco-Roman world between the sixth and fifth centuries BCE. These faiths and ritual practices demonstrated a deepening concern among their practitioners for personal immortality, accompanied by a sense of personal renewal through union with the divine. These initiates also strove to achieve regeneration by a symbolic enactment of the journey from death to rebirth through the underworld passage.

This dark descent and transformation is not, of course, limited to ancient tales. Perhaps no modern writer has ever had such a grasp of the mythic imagination as J.R.R. Tolkien, and Gandalf's transformation in *The Lord of the Rings* is certainly one of the most dramatic transformations in contemporary literature. At the Bridge of Khazad-dum, Gandalf the Grey battles with the Balrog of Moria, a huge, demonic being with enormous power, armed with a fiery sword and a many-thonged whip of flame. Balrogs are "Maiar," of the same order as Gandalf and the other most powerful wizards. However, evil forces have corrupted their powers, so Gandalf is facing his evil shadow. As they battle, Gandalf breaks the bridge under the Balrog, so that it falls into the chasm below. As it falls, however, the Balrog wraps its whip around Gandalf and drags him, too, into the pit. The two fall together for a long time, eventually landing in a subterranean lake, where their battle continues. After a long and furious battle, the Balrog is defeated, but this great ordeal causes Gandalf to die. He is sent back, however, and when he again appears in Middle-earth, he is transformed into Gandalf the White and has even greater powers.

[return]

The mythic hero does not typically return home to throngs of cheering fans. In fact, the returning hero may be changed beyond recognition. When Gandalf re-appears, the members of the Fellowship do not recognize him. This transformation is manifested on a divine scale when Jesus appears to his followers after his resurrection and is not recognized. Heroes also may return in disguise or limp back into town weak, weary, and covered with the dust of the road. However, mythic heroes do not return empty handed. One does not go to hell and back for nothing. This is another significant characteristic of mythic journeys. Though the hero may set out on a personal quest, the benefits or gifts with which heroes return are never for themselves alone. The shaman that has endured the trials of the underworld returns on the wings of a wild gander and is then able to rescue the souls of others.[21] When the quest is accomplished, the hero brings back some sort of life-transforming gift that renews "the community, the nation, the planet, or the ten thousand worlds."[22]

──────────────[amor and psyche]──────────────

It may seem odd that this discussion of the hero's journey has taken place without much mention of deities, but they have really been there all along. The influence of divine power on the hero's journey is depicted in many myths. One well-known story magnificently illustrates the many ways in which deities may become involved in a hero's quest. The story of Amor (also called Cupid) and Psyche is extremely complex, with multiple levels of natural, supernatural, and divine intervention as Psyche's journey develops.

In the interest of full disclosure, this story is not quite a myth. It is a story within a complex cycle of stories written by a second century CE Latin writer, Apuleius, in a novel entitled *Metamorphoses,* also known as the *Golden Ass.* However, the author was fluent in Greek and Latin and very well versed in the mythology of the Greeks and Romans, as well as the works of Virgil and Ovid. Certain aspects of the story vividly illustrate stages of the hero's journey while revealing many ways in which this journey is influenced by divine power. Though the text cannot be set out in full here, a discussion of these elements can enhance our understanding of the hero's journey while revealing more about the human/divine relationship. I have chosen to refer to the god of love as Amor, since Cupid has very different contemporary associations and may be misleading.

From the beginning of the story, the adventures of humans and gods are entwined. Psyche's departure from home and family is precipitated directly by the jealousy and resentment of Venus, who is more than a little annoyed that humans have begun to compare Psyche's beauty with her own. Jealous gods are nothing new, of course. In fact, one dominant mythic theme is divine resentment when humans deign to take on divine characteristics, whether this emulation is intentional or not. Psyche's beauty is certainly not her fault, but celestial characteristics are very dangerous for mortals, whether they are acquired intentionally (such as the knowledge of good and evil acquired by the first couple in the Garden of Eden) or completely by the accidents of birth. Immortality is especially reserved for divinity, and woe will come to all humans who seek to rise above their mortal condition.

In her rage over Psyche's impudent beauty, Venus orders her wild and headstrong son, Amor, to cause the lovely mortal to fall in love with a monster. Amorous power, however, is not easy to control, and her boy has his own desires. Psyche's real adventure begins when Zephyr, the West Wind, ever obedient to the god of love, takes her from the high precipice of her despair down into a divine valley, where she enters the palace of Amor. The lovely mortal dwells there completely oblivious to her divine surroundings, because she is blind to their powers. She receives sustenance from invisible servants and nightly visits from a lover whose face she is forbidden to see. Here, again, we find the myth of the forbidden thing, and here again (as with Izanagi in the underworld) it is knowledge (vision) that is forbidden to her.

In this transient state, Psyche cannot help but look back to a more familiar world. Even though Amor (whose identity she does not know) warns her against it, she greatly desires the comfort and company of her family. It is no surprise, given her state of blind innocence, that she falls for the cunning contrivances of her jealous sisters, who eventually convince her that she is wedded to a monstrous serpent and must destroy him.

In her remarkable analysis of the relationship between Psyche and her sisters, Christine Downing points out that the sisters function not only as shadows, but also as helpers in this story. Though they are motivated by envy, Psyche's sisters actually provide her with the boost she needs. While Amor would happily have "kept her in the dark," her sisters push her out of "naïve self-satisfaction toward a more conscious, individual loving."[23]

As with the first couple in the divine garden, Psyche's fate hangs in the balance. Will she remain in a state of blissful ignorance, or will she take a very dangerous peek into supernatural realms? We know what she will do. It is what mortals always do.

Psyche approaches her nightly visitor bearing an oil lamp and a blade, planning to reveal and then to destroy the monster. What she discovers is too much for her. In a moment of awakening as her light falls upon her husband's divine radiance, her ignorance is gone and so is her self-control. Pricked by his arrow and his beauty, she is overcome by paroxysms of desire and falls upon Amor, covering him with kisses. Interestingly, this does not wake him. Rather, he is aroused by one drop of oil from the lamp that falls on his shoulder, seriously wounding him. Of course, she has disobeyed and must face the consequences. Amor flies away. Psyche clings to his right leg for a time, but she has no gift of flight and finally must fall back to earth. Now her real hero's journey begins.

Aside from the gender role reversals, the story closely follows the traditional pattern of the hero's journey. There are obstacles to overcome and helpers who appear unexpectedly to guide her and provide assistance when all else has failed. Although the motifs of this story follow the familiar pattern, the gender issues are not irrelevant. Psyche's gradual awakening through her journey is a woman's awakening.[24] Stereotypical female characteristics also arise at various points. Especially at the early stages of her quest to find her beloved, Psyche tends to accept defeat too readily. She often contemplates suicide, only to be dissuaded from that drastic act by various intervening benefactors. The goddesses to whom she turns will not help her, however, fearing the wrath of their powerful sister goddess, and they instruct Psyche to confront Venus directly.

Finally, Psyche comes face-to-face with Venus, and the angry goddess assigns her all sorts of difficult tasks. With the help of various beings, Psyche succeeds in accomplishing these tasks, further angering the great goddess. Eventually, Venus sends Psyche on a mission to the underworld, hoping, it might be imagined, that this will finally rid her of this mortal pest. Meanwhile, Amor lies close to death, overcome by the tiny wound caused by his lover's betrayal. Psyche again receives assistance and guidance that enable her to accomplish the difficult and dangerous underworld journey. However, when she returns from her underworld trials bearing the box of beauty she has been ordered to deliver, Psyche cannot resist taking a peek inside the box. She sees no beauty within, but an infernal sleep arises from the box and overwhelms her.

At this point, Amor, who has recovered from his wound, intervenes on behalf of his mortal wife, wiping the sleep from her eyes and requesting Jupiter's assistance to overcome his mother's wrath. Jupiter grants immortality to Psyche and bestows his blessings on the couple, and they finally have a legitimate wedding ceremony. Though Venus and Psyche grudgingly forgive one another, one is left with the impression that this may not be the end of Psyche's mother-in-law troubles. Amor and Psyche have a child whose name is Pleasure (*voluptas*).

This myth, along with so many others, emphasizes the dynamic interaction between mortal and immortal, ignorance and wisdom, disobedience and courage. Between the divine and mortal worlds, there is a boundary. That dividing line separates the human world from the sacred realm, but it is also a place where they make contact—a place where they touch.

——————————————————————[gods]——————————————————————

Gods may remain in the background, bringing supernatural forces to bear in order to help or hinder the hero. They may intervene or simply watch and wait. The old, wise one standing on the corner and handing out cryptic advice may be a deity in disguise. Divine messengers are everywhere, as compassionate bodhisattvas and as vicious demons, as strangers seeking hospitality and as beautiful saboteurs set on the path to distract or torment the traveler.

As already mentioned, early primal cultures did not separate the spiritual dimension from the rest of the world, so any adventure included the participation of spiritual powers. These spirits sometimes took animal form, since the symbolism of these cultures emphasized interconnectedness with all forms of life. Deities were often depicted as part animal or as accompanied by animals, and the imagery and function of one deity often blended or merged with another. Over many thousands of years, however, distinct deities emerge with specific powers and realms of authority. The relationship that develops between gods and humans greatly influences the path of the hero's journey and the spiritual life of humanity.

the female divine

It is likely that the very earliest archaeological evidence depicts the divine as female. As scholars have become more aware of the mounting evidence, a debate has developed regarding the significance of these female images. Since Maria Gimbutas's pioneering archaeological work in ancient goddess imagery, the idea of pervasive worship of the Great Goddess has taken hold, along with theories regarding the rise and fall of associated matrifocal or matriarchal cultures in the Paleolithic and Neolithic periods. Others have challenged the theory that worship of the Great Goddess was nearly universal, and charged that the early material record is much more complex and diverse. It is important to note that reading the artifacts of preliterate cultures is always a dicey business. The incredible variety among images related to the goddess makes this task even more difficult. One enormous contribution of Gimbutas's work is in the analysis, cataloguing, and grouping of these images.[25]

Without entering into the debate here, it seems clear that many early cultures worshipped at least one goddess. This does not necessarily imply the existence of worldwide Mother Goddess worship, and it certainly does not automatically indicate that earlier cultures were more egalitarian and less patriarchal (though some such cultures may well have existed). However, evidence suggests that goddess worship was extensive among ancient cultures, and the relationships that developed between human and divine took on characteristics emerging from this "Great Mother" imagery.

The reasons for representing the divine as female were undoubtedly complex, but some associations seem obvious. What primal people observed was that life-blood poured from women periodically and, unlike warriors or hunters who suffered or died when this occurred, women were unharmed. They also noted that women sometimes grew large, like the moon, new life poured from their bodies in a wave of water and blood, and then their bodies returned to their former state. Furthermore, milk to sustain this new life came from the breast of the mother. It is no surprise, therefore, that early humans associated the powers of life, sustenance, and death with the female.

Christine Downing notes early evidence associating worship of the Great Mother with nurturing, especially with the provision of food. "What first inspires worship is that there is food; the first focus of worship is the source of food."[26] Therefore, early artifacts associate the female with primal power. "She is at the very center of what is sacred and necessary."[27] Since correspondences between goddesses and their human counterparts were typically more direct than was characteristic of their male counterparts, the corporeal aspect of the goddess was never completely subsumed by the spiritual. Thus, observing the female's power to bring and nurture life, it was not much of a leap "to recognize the goddess also as creatrix—mother of all that is—and thus to view the universe as a woman giving birth to all forms of life."[28]

Goddesses were also very frequently symbolized in terms of triads. Recent scholarship has focused on the three-fold goddess as maiden (or virgin), mother, and crone, associated with waxing, full, and waning phases of the moon.[29] Another triad frequently associated with the goddess is that of life, death, and regeneration, the primordial cycle of the mythic worldview.[30] Although there is evidence that certain goddesses were specifically associated with each of these phases of the cycle, many goddesses possessed powers associated with multiple roles, and some goddesses almost certainly simultaneously represented life and death as well as rebirth and regeneration. "The goddess's cyclic disappearances and reappearances are closely connected to her association with increase and decrease, protection and desertion, vision and lunacy, creation and destruction, life and death, feast and famine. What she gives she also takes away."[31]

Among these goddesses, one of the most powerful and significant is Kali. First appearing in the popular Hindu text, the *Mahabharata,* she eventually comes to hold a very high place in tantric iconography, text, and ritual. She is strongly associated with *shakti* energy, a form of female energy considered to be the fundamental creative power of the universe. Though she is depicted in many forms, in her fierce aspect she is black, naked, and bloodthirsty, with a protruding tongue dripping blood, a necklace of skulls, a belt made of human hands, and a raised sword. As Kali, the devourer, she represents death, destruction, and the consuming aspects of reality. However, Kali also is portrayed as young and beautiful, fully dressed in lovely garments, with a gentle smile and hands that gesture reassuringly. In this aspect, her maternal characteristics are emphasized, and she symbolizes triumph over death.

Hecate, associated with Greco-Roman culture, is another polymorphous deity. She is an ancient goddess, with pre-Olympian roots, and her symbolic manifestations and associations are extremely complex. Although she is strongly associated with childbirth and nurturing the young, she also is associated with magic, witchcraft, and the underworld. She is a dark figure, goddess of crossroads, depicted in later antiquity as a triple-formed goddess facing in three directions, sometimes with animal heads such as a dog, serpent, and horse. She is most frequently portrayed as accompanied by one or more dogs, and a common form of offering to her was to leave meat at a crossroads. Homer and Hesiod portray her as a great goddess, honored by the gods with powers on earth and heaven, as well as the sea. She is especially praised for her abilities to increase livestock and to nurse and help raise the young, especially young men. However, she also became associated with ghosts, underworld spirits, and sorcery. Her image was placed at gates and doorways, because she was believed to have power over the spirits of the dead. Hecate is the "tender-hearted," offering comfort to Demeter over the loss of her daughter. She is also the "she-bitch," accompanied by ghost hounds that bark to announce her presence.

However she appears, no matter what role she assumes, the imagery of the goddess is often cyclical and dynamic. Gimbutas summarizes these themes:

> The main theme of Goddess symbolism is the mystery of birth and death and the renewal of life, not only human but all life on earth and indeed in the whole cosmos. ... She was the single source of all life who took her energy from the springs and wells, from the sun, moon, and moist earth.[32]

All these images and themes attempt to articulate the presence and power of the goddess, but finally, they fall short. This is the great irony of the divine presence in any form. Images and ideas can never be enough.

There is another facet to this mystery as well that may be specific to her female nature—the goddess touches us, her stories live in us, she brings us into a profound sense of connectedness, and we can never quite articulate how and why. In an account of her own goddess quest, Carol Christ expresses it this way: "Present in the rocks that undergird life, in the darkness where life is conceived and transformed, in the air and the ever-changing waters, the Goddess is the love that supports embodied and relational being."[33]

The earliest symbols of goddess worship reflected mythical rather than linear time, and her earliest imagery reflected the dynamic motion of swirling spirals and close associations with creatures such as birds, serpents, and even hedgehogs. As her imagery expanded, she assumed multiple roles and personalities, but her deepest meanings may always be shrouded in mystery, shining and unattainable at the bottom of her dark pools.

the male divine

The divine male takes his time overcoming the power and authority of the goddess, but he arrives on the scene early in human history. Archaeological exploration has unearthed male as well as female images, along with a great many artifacts with no discernible gender. While goddesses are often associated with natural imagery or reproductive and seasonal cycles, male deities are more often associated with their activities or roles.[34] Some early depictions of the male divine, typically from cultures practicing agriculture and domestication of animals, represent him as the son or consort of the goddess. Later, heavenly pantheons are filled with male and female deities, who make love and war with one another and compete for power, love, and human attention. Eventually, especially in monotheistic traditions with written scripture, imagery of the female all but disappears from human depictions of the divine, and the almighty male takes center stage.

Many ancient cultures associated the male divine with the sky, and Eliade suggests that some of the earliest human worship may have been directed toward a celestial being who created the universe and assures its fecundity by pouring seminal rain upon it.[35] It is clear that the image of sky father is a recurring theme in mythology, often paired with an earth mother. Eliade associates this sky imagery with certain celestial traits: "The sky 'symbolizes' transcendence, power and changelessness simply by being there. It exists because it is high, infinite, immovable, powerful."[36] Therefore, the Most High God takes on these characteristics. "The regions above man's reach, the starry places, are invested with the divine majesty of the transcendent, of absolute reality, of everlastingness."[37] Since the heavens are inaccessible to humanity, they belong to supernatural powers and beings. Unlike goddesses who assumed forms associated with human and animal fecundity, the sky gods were typically supreme, inaccessible, and aloof. When they did interact with humans, it was often through an intermediary, very often a son.

The father god's strong association with male fertility underscores his role as providing the form and direction of the creation. "Even as the divine seed awakens and gives shape to life, the father-god's commandments, principles, and laws organize and direct the energies of his creation."[38]

In some pantheons, individual deities represent the various stages of the mythic cycle. In the Hindu tradition, for example, Brahma is the creator of the universe as well as the progenitor of humanity. He is one of the *Trimurti,* the three forms of the divine, the others being Vishnu, the maintainer or preserver, and Siva, the destroyer or transformer. Although they are sometimes represented as three heads on one neck, each deity has an individual mythology and rituals associated with him.

However, the motif of the dying and rising god is probably the most common divine representation of the cycle of life, death, and regeneration. Though there are a few examples of female deities associated with this cycle, such as Persephone and Ishtar, the vast majority of these deities are male.

Long before Christianity emerged, deities were born (sometimes to virgins), suffered death or some form of death-like experience, passed through an underworld journey, and emerged reborn, either literally or symbolically. Often, though not always, this death was associated with a divine sacrifice made for the well-being or salvation of humanity. This imagery ranges from Australian aboriginal mythology to the ancient Sumerians to North American indigenous traditions. One significant example of dying and rising imagery can be found in the Egyptian myth of Osiris, discussed at greater length in the following chapters. Well-known examples outside of Christianity also include Mithras, Tammuz, Dionysus, and Odin. Though there is considerable debate, many scholars would also place Jesus in this category.

When these gods are reborn, they are typically transformed in the process. Sometimes the transformation is so great that the divine one no longer assumes human form. Adonis, originally a Phoenician deity, also appears in Greek and Roman mythology. He is gored by a wild boar, and at his death Venus sprinkles his blood with nectar. From this combination comes the fragile windflower, or anemone. In his epic narrative poem, *Metamorphoses,* the Roman poet Ovid describes a number of these transformations.

As with ancient goddesses who were worshipped both as creators and destroyers of the world, these male deities also represent multiple natures, complex social associations, and even more complex networks of cult, ritual, and worship. For example, Osiris, the Egyptian god of the living and the dead, judges souls at the entrance to the underworld. Though the cult of Osiris was associated with funerary rites, Osiris also symbolized forces of nature and immortality.

monotheism

The male deity is, of course, most firmly associated with all known monotheistic traditions. The evolution of monotheism (the worship of only one divine being) is complex, and theories abound regarding its origins and development. Most scholars, however, believe that current monotheistic traditions developed out of earlier cultures worshipping more than one deity. There is significant historical and scriptural evidence that emergence of monotheism in the Abrahamic traditions (Judaism, Christianity, Islam, Baha'i) was preceded by polytheistic traditions and was influenced by views of other cultures such as Egypt and Syria. Additionally, monotheism tended to develop gradually out of *henotheism,* the worship of a single god while accepting the existence of other deities or heavenly beings. In the ancient Near East, each major city had a patron deity, and nomadic people traveled with their tribal gods. Many scholars believe that in Genesis 1:26,[39] when God says "let us make humankind in our image, according to our likeness," he is addressing a heavenly council.

There is also considerable debate about what tradition initiated monotheism. Some scholars refer to the Aten cult during the reign of the pharaoh Akhenaton in Egypt as the first manifestation of monotheism in the ancient Near East. By the Late Bronze Age, the cult of Marduk had also elevated him from patron god of Babylon to a universal supreme being. Others focus on Ahura Mazda, the supreme deity in Zoroastrianism. Though he is dualistically paired with an evil deity, Angra Mainyu, it seems clear that Zoroastrians recognized Ahura Mazda as the supreme being, just as Christians affirm God's power over Satan. Zoroastrianism was once one of the largest religions on earth, and many scholars suggest that this tradition had a significant influence on Christianity, as well as other world religions.

It is likely that several traditions developed monotheistic views at or near the same time, influenced by motifs and narratives from a variety of sources. By the second and third centuries of the common era, various competing religious movements advocated some form of monotheism or *monolatrism* (recognition of the existence of many gods while worshipping only one). Cults devoted to Apollo, Dionysus, Marduk and Mithra all proclaimed their deities as supreme, viewing the gods of other polytheistic traditions as mere manifestations or servants of the one god.

Although the idea of worshipping one god may seem straightforward and absolute, there are many different manifestations of monotheistic belief, from the trinitarian monotheism of Christianity to Hindu monistic belief that all the various gods are actually manifestations of one non-personal divine reality. While Judaism and Islam understand God's oneness as absolute, other traditions hold the pantheistic belief that the whole universe is divine, but deny the existence of any divine being outside nature.

The character of the one God also is variously understood, even within traditions. Of course, an absolute and transcendent deity can only be partially understood within any human community, so traditions have implemented various methods to symbolically represent the divine. Myths often utilize *anthropomorphism,* the use of human characteristics, to symbolize aspects of the divine nature. For example, in Genesis 3:8, God strolls in the garden in the cool of the evening and carries on an extended chat with his disobedient children.

The monotheistic traditions utilized many masculine metaphors for God, including father, king, shepherd, lord, and warrior. Even Christian monotheism, however, has not always represented God as strictly male. Early church leaders such as Augustine and Anselm, for example, wrote prayers that incorporated female imagery for the divine. Anselm's song celebrating the mother love of Christ is an extraordinary example:

> Jesus, as a mother you gather your people to you:
> You are gentle with us as a mother with her children;
> Often you weep over our sins and our pride:
> tenderly you draw us from hatred and judgment.
> You comfort us in sorrow and bind up our wounds:
> in sickness you nurse us,
> and with pure milk you feed us.[40]

the gods of undoing

As we have seen, the mythic worldview encompasses and embraces all aspects of the cycle: death as well as life, chaos as well as order. Processes such as decline and decay are part of the transformational process, and have the potential to release great power that can be used for new creative events or activities. Some ancient cultures incorporated these powers into their rituals and directed their worship toward the deities responsible for them.

One such being is the trickster. Most ancient images of this divine troublemaker represent him as an amoral phallic figure with an overactive sex drive. However, the trickster's phallic nature also underscores his creativity, and he is often regarded as the creator or assistant to the creator. Trickster deities represent defiance of social boundaries and the powers of chaos. Some familiar examples are Coyote and Raven in North American mythology and Maui in Polynesia, as well as the Sumerian deity, Enki, the Norse Loki, and the Hindu Krishna. The Greeks and Romans related myths in which gods destroyed the natural order or initiated great battles and upheavals.

Hermes, messenger of the gods, also was known as a cunning robber, cattle driver, bringer of dreams, watcher by night, and thief at the gates. One story relates that, on the day of his birth, he first invented the lyre and later stole cattle from his half-brother, Apollo, covering up the footprints of the sacred herd through trickery. When Apollo accused him of the theft, he denied it (some call this the First Lie), and his mother, Maia, attempted to protect him. Zeus, however, entered the argument and revealed that Hermes was indeed the thief. The clever demigod began to play the lyre and so enchanted Zeus that he allowed Hermes to keep the cattle in exchange for giving the lyre to Apollo. One version of this story relates that Zeus also rewarded Hermes for his cleverness by granting him full Olympian status and giving him gifts to mark his status as messenger of the gods: a round hat, a beribboned staff, and winged sandals. Zeus's brother, Hades, also accepted Hermes as his messenger, and he became the one to summon the dead into the underworld.[41] He was known as a psychopomp, one who could travel freely between the upper world and the netherworld.

Although the trickster is predominantly depicted as male, there are some significant females who also fall into this category. Eris is the Greek goddess of strife and discord. She is best known for casting a golden apple marked "for the fairest" among the celebrants at a wedding party, starting a quarrel among the great goddesses that eventually led to the Trojan War. More pleasant, though no less inclined to trickery, are the goddesses of mirth, laughter, and jest. The Japanese goddess, Uzume, is best known for tricking the great sun goddess into emerging from a cave, thus returning light to the world. Baubo, a Greek goddess, was the only one able to make Demeter smile as she wandered the world mourning for her lost daughter. Like the male trickster deities, these goddesses are fun loving, bawdy, and sexually liberated, but they also are associated with wisdom and healing.

[the power of three]

The hero's transformation in the underworld, the shamanic ordeal of death and rebirth, even the various symbolic representations of the divine, all have a very strong association with the number three. A death that lasts three days, corresponding to the dark of the moon, is a very frequent motif in myths and rituals that relate and reenact stories of death, underworld travel, and renewal. Eliade suggests that this lunar symbolism of the moon dying and being reborn three days later "stresses the idea that death is the first condition of all mystical regeneration."[42] When a deity descends into the underworld, all the cycles of nature cease, and heaven grieves. The mythical ascent of the deity not only involves the rebirth of the god, but also the regeneration of the whole natural world.

We already have noted that goddess imagery was often represented in triad form. Ancient Romans devoted several temples to the worship of divine triads such as Jupiter, Juno, and Minerva. In addition to the Hindu triad discussed above, the Greeks, Sumerians, Egyptians, and Mayans also worshipped the divine in three-fold form, as do some neopagan traditions. The Christian trinity retains this three-fold form in the imagery of the three persons of God but maintains that they are completely united in one divine Godhead.

We conclude these adventures of gods and heroes with yet another mystery. The cycle of the hero's journey is not merely cyclical. Like the mythic cycle it represents, the hero's journey is transformative. Otherwise, what would the journey be for? The hero who returns is not the hero who departed, but a new being, born of the trials and transformations inherent in boundary crossings into the unknown. Likewise, the place to which the hero returns is not the same old starting place. Rather, the place of the beginning has become a place of recognition, of new understanding and new hope. The cyclical pattern of the journey turns out not to be a circle but a spiral, spinning infinitely out of the past and into adventures as yet unknown. Achieving this transformation, however, is never a simple task.

[chapter]

THE UNDERWORLD

If you are going through hell, keep going.

Winston Churchill

It may be wise to pause here and take a breath. Of all the thresholds mythical travelers must cross, none is as dangerous and unpredictable as this dark passage. Those who take the underworld journey typically turn in that direction when there is no other option. It is the land of no return. The underworld is also, however, the ultimate location of transformation.

From as early as the fourth millennium BCE, mythical narratives have included references to the dismal realm of the dead, a land from which escape is only possible by extraordinary means. Such expressions have occurred in myriad forms and in diverse locations and periods of history. Into these nether regions, an array of heroes and deities descend. The stories of the great descent vary greatly, depending on the way the destination is understood.

Most scholars agree that the very first human rituals centered on the issue of death. Neanderthal gravesites indicate that even these early ancestors buried their dead with apparent concern for the next world. These ritual burials were very likely also associated with sacrifice, and some ancient sites appear to indicate belief in rebirth.[1] Accounts of a land of the dead exist wherever cultures hold the belief that death is not final and absolute. These images appear to be fundamental to human spiritual metaphor—as death is fundamental to human existence.

Myths centering on the descent into the underworld sometimes bring the certainty of death into contact with the promise of rebirth or regeneration. Deities of the underworld, therefore, were often associated or identified with gods of the harvest. Osiris, Demeter, Proserpina, and Freya, among others, are associated both with death and fertility. Among the Ibo people of West Africa, the goddess, Ala, rules the underworld, receiving the dead in her pocket or womb, but she is also protector of the harvest and the deity who makes humans and animals fertile.

Karen Armstrong summarizes this perspective in her discussion of the Eleusinian mysteries, secret rites associated with Demeter, goddess of the grain and also Mistress of the Dead. "Death was fearful, frightening and inevitable, but it was not the end." Just as seeds must die in order to produce grain, and pruning encourages new growth, "confrontation with death led to spiritual regeneration and was a form of human pruning." Though only the gods are immortal, such rituals enabled participants to live more fearlessly and to face death as a necessary part of the transformative process. These myths and rituals "helped people to accept their mortality, to pass on to the next stage, and to have the courage to change and grow."[2]

On the other hand, the immortality of the individual soul was not the emphasis in this association. The dead descended into the netherworld and remained there. Though early understanding of the underworld did not see it as a place of punishment (or reward), humans were mortal, and death was final. The association between death and fertility, exemplified by deities who represented both, affirmed the mythic cycle through which death and life were intertwined.

Before considering the myths of underworld descent, it is necessary to look more deeply into the abyss itself. The most common understanding of the underworld is a realm, usually under the surface of the earth, where souls travel after death. It may simply be a land of shadows. Especially in later mythological visions, it may be a place of eternal punishment, the dark alternative reserved for souls that are not sanctified. Underworld geographies varied, and some cultures distinguished realms of the dead from areas designated for punishment or reward.

Whether the underworld is understood as a place of transformation or of eternal suffering depends in large part on the way a particular culture understands time and history. As we have seen, when we focus on the mythical worldview, divine history is understood as a cyclical transition from birth through growth, decline, death, transformation, and rebirth. These traditions are more likely to understand the underworld as a place of transformation or transition to another state. Van der Leeuw observes that in cyclical time "every sunrise is a victory over chaos, every festival a cosmic beginning, every sowing a new creation, every holy place a foundation of the cosmos...."[3] Thus, the successive revelations necessary for rebirth are acquired through a process that includes ritual death and a return to chaos.[4] On the other hand, linear divine histories such as those that eventually developed in the Abrahamic traditions came to understand the netherworld in terms of eternal suffering. In many traditions, concepts of the underworld journey changed over time.

Some of the oldest traditions understood the underworld simply as an abode of the dead, associated neither with transformation nor with punishment. The House of Darkness (also called the House of Dust) in the Sumerian epic of Gilgamesh is a dry, dreary place where the dead live in darkness, eating dust and clay, wearing garments of feathers. Though the spirits of the dead may be recognized, they are only pale and powerless shadows of their former selves. Another Sumerian name for the underworld was *kur*, the void space between the primeval sea and the earth that served as the home of the dead. *Sheol* (Hebrew for grave or pit) was understood by the early Hebrews to be the land where the dead gathered. Though not a place of punishment, it also was viewed as a land of shadows, a dark and gloomy place associated with sorrow. Later Rabbinical and early Christian cultures contrasted this neutral resting place with *Gehenna*, a place where the wicked go for punishment. Since English Bibles traditionally translated both *Sheol* and *Gehenna* with the Anglo Saxon term "hell," the distinction between the two realms was lost in the English-speaking world.

For the Greeks, the equivalent of Sheol was Hades (also called *Erebus*). The term is used both to describe the underworld and to refer to its lord or ruler. In older Greek myth, the realm of Hades is very much like Sheol, a gloomy or misty place where mortals travel after death. The idea of judgment was not present in the early mythology but develops in later Greek philosophy. In classic Greek and Roman mythology, there are several underworld realms, including the Elysian Fields, resting place of heroic and virtuous souls, and *Tartarus,* the pit of torment and suffering. These realms are separated from the world of the living by five rivers.

The underworld myths and rituals of ancient Egypt were particularly complex. The Egyptian land of the dead was called *Duat,* a dark and dangerous realm filled with lakes of fire through which every Egyptian must pass after death. Tombs, mummifications, and various spells and rituals were all designed to assist the deceased through the difficult transitions that were understood to take place after death. Eventually, however, the underworld traveler must confront Osiris, Lord of Eternity and head of the court of judgment in the Hall of the Two Truths. The jackal-headed Anubis and Toth, great mediator between good and evil, preside over a ritual in which the feather-symbol of Truth is weighed against the heart of the deceased. If the heart is at least as light as the feather, the traveler has passed the test. Next to the scales stands *Amemit,* a fierce female demon with the head of a crocodile, the body of a hippopotamus, and the legs of a lioness. The deceased who balance the scales move on to the Field of Rushes (also called the Field of Offerings), an everlasting paradise. Those who fail are given over to the Devouring Monster.

The concept of underworld judgment could be extreme. For the Maya, only those who died a violent death could enter heaven. All others entered *Xibalba,* the place of fright, ruled by the Mayan death gods, a terrifying place of trials and torments, where all who failed the tests suffered excruciating torment. The Aztecs also viewed the layers of the underworld as filled with dangers. Souls who entered had to descend through the layers, facing the dangers of each layer as they passed.

Asian cultures also maintained underworld traditions, sometimes extremely complex. In Japan, the underworld realm was called Yomi, land of night or gloom. This realm was completely empty until Izanami, the goddess creator described in Chapter Two, died giving birth to the god of fire. The thunder gods that grew from the maggots on her body took up residence in Yomi and tormented the wicked, while Izanami remained as queen of the underworld. The Buddhist understanding of the lands of the dead became particularly intricate and will be discussed in greater detail later in this chapter.

Characteristics of the underworld also varied, though certain features frequently appear. Perhaps most notably, the passage to the dark realm is a one-way path. The underworld is repeatedly described as the land of no return. In the epic of Gilgamesh, the House of Darkness is the house where those who enter do not come out, along the road of no return. For the Babylonians and Sumerians, the underworld is always the land from which no traveler returns. Other prominent features include some form of passage or entrance (often a cave, well, or pit), a barrier or threshold of some kind, a gatekeeper or guard, and layers or levels through which the traveler must pass. Access to Hades, for example, typically involved crossing the river Styx, carried across by Charon, the ferryman. Once one crossed the river, one had to get past Cerberus, the three-headed dog that guards the underworld. Another common image is that of the underworld as a mirror image of the upper world, identical except that it is upside down or in reverse. In these lands, the occupants may do things in reverse from the ordinary world or may live according to different rules.

There are also certain themes that recur in mythology relating to the underworld journey. When a living god or mortal enters the underworld, it is very often to recover a loved one. Orpheus, the Greek hero, descends in order to find his wife, Eurydice. Izanagi, as we have seen, takes the journey to reclaim his wife so that they can continue with creation together. Similar stories appear in Chinese Buddhism and among some African peoples, including the Ashanti.

In other accounts, the traveler descends into the underworld following some command, often accompanied by a set of careful instructions. Psyche makes the journey on the command of Venus, and Aeneas goes to seek his father, following the command of his father's ghost. Odysseus makes the journey to seek counsel from the dead. In order to accomplish the twelfth and most dangerous of the tasks assigned to him by Eurystheus, Hercules travels to the underworld to capture Cerberus.

Not all underworld journeys are intentional. In most versions of the story of Demeter and Persephone, the young goddess is abducted by Hades, lord of the underworld, and taken below. The grieving mother puts sufficient pressure on Zeus to obtain her daughter's release, but Persephone must still return to the underworld for a period of time each year.

[inanna]

One of the earliest myths describing the underworld journey relates the descent of the goddess Inanna into the kingdom of the dead. Her reasons for undertaking the descent are somewhat obscure, but the description of her journey evokes some of the most powerful symbolic themes related to the underworld descent. Joseph Campbell refers to this myth as the "oldest recorded account of the passage through the gates of metamorphosis."[5]

Inanna, sometimes called Queen of Heaven, was the most important goddess in the Sumerian pantheon in ancient Mesopotamia. Her many temples and shrines, including the "house of heaven" at Uruk, were scattered along the Tigris and Euphrates rivers. She is most strongly associated with sexual love and fertility, and there is evidence that sexual rites reenacting the sacred marriage were commonly practiced in her temples. However, she is also one of the Sumerian war deities and is believed to possess immense power. Her symbol is the eight-pointed star, and she is commonly associated with lions, sometimes depicted as standing on the backs of two lionesses. As with so many ancient deities, her name, ancestry, and the details of her story vary from tradition to tradition.

The myths of Inanna may have been created any time between 3500 and 1900 BCE, and the tale of her underworld descent is related in a relatively intact set of thirty clay tablets and fragments, consisting of more than 400 lines of text and inscribed around 1750 BCE. The story of her underworld descent begins with a simple declaration: "From the Great Above, Inanna opened her ear to the Great Below."[6] The Sumerian words for ear and for wisdom are identical, so Inanna's decision to pursue the underworld journey is also pursuit of greater understanding. "It is the Great Below, and the knowledge of death and rebirth, life and stasis, that will make of Inanna an 'Honored Counselor' and a guide to the land."[7]

Though many accounts and interpretations focus on the details of her descent into the underworld, her activities and concerns leading up to her journey also are critical to the symbolic meaning of the story. When Inanna chooses to abandon heaven and earth and her holy temples in order to descend to the underworld, she makes extensive preparations before she even begins her descent.

In order to understand the imagery of her preparations more fully, it is necessary to consider the Sumerian concept of *me*. In Sumerian mythology, *me* are universal decrees of divine authority, invoked to develop arts, crafts, and civilization. Though they are sometimes understood as blueprints or tablets, they also are associated in Sumerian mythology with various specific objects. The *me* granted power over these aspects of civilization and may also have brought them into existence. There were hundreds of them, representing all aspects of culture, both positive and negative, and the god of culture, Enki, kept them in his holy city of Eridu. One myth relates how Inanna goes to visit Enki, protesting that she has been given insufficient power. Eventually, Enki becomes drunk, and Inanna manages to persuade him to give her hundreds of *me*. She then immediately departs by boat for her own city of Uruk. Once he is sober, Enki regrets his gift and sends a mighty sea monster to stop her. However, she is able to escape, and eventually Enki allows her to keep the gifted *me*.

Interestingly, the narrative of Inanna's underworld journey pays considerable attention to her attire and the way in which she arrays herself for the journey. In the tale, seven *me* are associated with specific articles of clothing or symbols of power. As she prepares to make her journey, she attires herself from top to bottom with these symbols. She places a crown on her head, arranges her hair across her forehead, wraps herself in her royal robe and breastplate, chooses jewelry and applies makeup, and takes up a gold ring and a lapis measuring rod and line. On the surface of the story, Inanna prepares for her journey simply by carefully getting dressed, arranging her hair and makeup, and taking up certain objects. In fact, she is clothing herself in the cultural powers associated with her realm in the Great Above.

This connection between female dress and power is also a familiar symbol.[8] A common motif in Phoenician ivory carvings is the so-called "woman at the window," depicting a beautiful woman with an Egyptian style headdress, sometimes wearing a crown, hairpiece, or necklace, and gazing frontally out of a window. In 2 Kings 2:9, Jezebel, a Phoenician princess, prepares to confront Jehu by painting her eyes and arranging her hair before seating herself at the window. Women's hair dressing and cosmetic applications have been likened to putting on their armor for battle. The point here may be that one should not underestimate the power of a woman fully arrayed. If that female is a goddess, preparing herself to undertake an underworld journey, there is no doubt that she takes the dangers of her travels very seriously.

Her awareness of the dangers she is likely to confront is also evident in another aspect of her preparations. As she sets out, she is accompanied by her companion, Ninshubur, who serves as her minister and faithful servant. In terms of the hero's journey motifs, Ninshubur functions in this story as the faithful sidekick who can be counted upon in times of grave danger. Interestingly, Inanna refers to Ninshubur not only as a servant and an advisor but also as a companion in battle. She advises Ninshubur of her travel plans and then gives her very specific instructions to follow should Inanna fail to return. As she continues on her way, Inanna stops and turns back to Ninshubur one last time: "Go now, Ninshubur—Do not forget the words I have commanded you."[9] In the symbolic language of myth, the events to come are anticipated in these first instructions to Ninshubur. Those who hear the story now realize that Inanna will not return, and they also know that at that point everything will depend on Ninshubur's strength and loyalty.

Though her power in the Great Above is beyond question, Inanna may not enter the Great Below without permission. At the outer gates, she knocks loudly and calls upon the gatekeeper, Neti, the chief gatekeeper of the *kur,* advising him that she is alone and wishes to enter. Neti replies by asking that quintessential question of the crossroads: "Who are you?" She identifies herself as Inanna, Queen of Heaven, and indicates that she is on her way to the East.

This association between the underworld and the East is somewhat startling, since the eastern direction is obviously associated with the rising of the sun and therefore typically connected to the return of light and life rather than death and the underworld. In Sumerian mythology, the word *"kur"* also means land or mountain and was often associated with the Zagros Mountains to the east of Sumer. Since the term was also associated with the underworld realm, perhaps these mountains were related to the realm of the dead.

As Neti inquires about the reason for her journey, he clearly indicates the nature of the threshold over which she seeks to step: "Why has your heart led you on the road from which no traveler returns?"[10] Inanna's answer is somewhat obscure. She first mentions her older sister, Ereshkigal, queen of the underworld. Then she indicates that she has come to witness the funeral rites of her sister's husband, Gugalanna. However, although her encounter with Ereshkigal is at the very center of the story, there is no more mention of Gugalanna, his death, or his funeral in this narrative. At any rate, it is worth noting that Inanna is certainly not dressed for a funeral.

Neti then goes to the palace of Ereshkigal, Queen of the Underworld, to deliver Inanna's message. It is unlikely that he was not immediately aware of the visitor's identity, since he describes her as a maid "as tall as heaven, as wide as the earth, as strong as the foundations of the city wall," and then proceeds to set out in elaborate detail all the preparations Inanna has made for her visit.[11] There is no question that Ereshkigal recognizes this description of her younger sister, since she reacts by slapping her thigh and biting her lip, gestures that certainly imply some strong emotional reaction. Ereshkigal then takes the matter into her heart and devises a plan.

She instructs Neti to bolt the seven gates of the underworld and then, one by one, to open each gate a crack and allow Inanna to enter. As she enters each gate, Neti is to remove her royal garments. She finishes her instructions with a grim proclamation: "Let the holy priestess of heaven enter bowed low."[12]

The text that follows is highly repetitive and ritualistic. After bolting the gates, Neti opens the outer gate and tells Inanna to enter. When she enters the first gate, he removes her crown. When she asks, "What is this?" he replies, "Quiet, Inanna, the ways of the underworld are perfect. They may not be questioned." At each of the following gates, he removes another of her royal garments, and the question and answer are exactly the same. At the seventh gate, Neti removes her royal robe, so that she does, in fact, enter Ereshkigal's throne room naked and bowed low.

The confrontation between Inanna and Ereshkigal is a classic face-to-face encounter. Ereshkigal rises from her throne. Inanna starts toward the throne. However, there is little suspense, since Ereshkigal's actions are brutal and swift. The Anunnaki, judges of the underworld, surround Inanna and pass judgment on her. Then Ereshkigal fastens the eye of death on Inanna, speaks the word of wrath against her, and utters the cry of guilt. She then strikes her, and the effect is immediate. "Inanna was turned into a corpse, a piece of rotting meat, and was hung from a hook on the wall."[13]

Were this not a mythic account, the story might end here with the victory of death over an impetuous and foolish goddess. However, in the mythic realm, death is not the end of anything. Inanna's fate now depends upon the courage and loyalty of her faithful servant. When Inanna has not returned after three days and three nights, Ninshubur begins to carry out Inanna's instructions. First, she performs the appropriate rituals of mourning for her divine queen. She then sets out to visit the holy shrines of the patriarchal deities, Enlil, Nanna, and, finally, Enki. Wording her request in the ritual language as Inanna has instructed, she begs for their assistance, crying out, "Do not let the holy priestess of heaven be put to death in the underworld."[14]

The responses of Enlil and Nanna are typical of wrathful fathers, advising their rebellious offspring that they must reap what they sow. They both reply with anger:

> My daughter craved the Great Above.
> Inanna craved the Great Below.
> She who receives the me of the underworld does not return.
> She who goes to the Dark City stays there.[15]

When Ninshubur seeks Enki at the temple of Eridu and makes the same request, however, Enki's response calls forth another fatherly image—that of the grieving father who will do anything at all to save his daughter, regardless of what foolishness or disobedience may have led her into danger.

> What has happened?
> What has my daughter done?
> Inanna! Queen of All the Land! Holy Priestess of Heaven!
> I am troubled. I am grieved.[16]

For such a rescue operation, great armies of heroes and deities have no chance. From the dirt under his fingernails, Enki creates two tiny, genderless creatures and carefully instructs them about their mission. He gives them the food and water of life and tells them to sneak into the underworld under the door. Once there, he advises them, they will find the queen of the underworld "moaning with the cries of a woman about to give birth." He instructs them to reply to her cries and moans with their own sympathetic cries. Obeying Enki's instructions exactly, the tiny beings find Ereshkigal just as they expected to find her, crying out in pain. In what is probably an unintentionally humorous ritual, the little beings respond to every cry of the dark goddess with cries of their own.

Impressed with their compassion, Ereshkigal offers them her blessing, along with a gift. When she offers the water-gift and the grain-gift, they decline. She has no idea, of course, that they already possess these gifts and have been carrying them all along. Finally, she asks them what they desire, and they respond, "We wish only the corpse that hangs from the hook on the wall."[17] When Ereshkigal indicates that the corpse belongs to Inanna, they still insist, and the corpse is given to them. They then sprinkle the food and water of life upon the corpse. Inanna arises.

As Inanna prepares to ascend back to the upper world, the judges of the underworld seize her and advise that no one "ascends from the underworld unmarked."[18] She is instructed that she must provide someone to replace her in the underworld, and as she ascends the demons of the underworld cling to her. When Inanna comes upon Ninshubur, still waiting in her mourning clothes outside the palace gates, Ninshubur throws herself at Inanna's feet. The demons indicate that they will take Ninshubur as Inanna's substitute, but the Queen of Heaven cries out on behalf of her faithful companion and advisor, refusing to give her to the demons. In a similar manner, Inanna speaks on behalf of her sons, as they, too, throw themselves at Inanna's feet, and she refuses to surrender them to the demons. Finally, by a big apple tree in Uruk, the group comes upon Dumuzi, Inanna's husband. Unlike the others, he is dressed in shining garments and sitting on a magnificent throne. He makes no move to greet or recognize her. Immediately, the demons seize him.

> Inanna fastened on Dumuzi the eye of death.
> She spoke against him the word of wrath.
> She uttered against him the cry of guilt:
> "Take him! Take Dumuzi away!"[19]

The story does not end here, but Inanna's ascent from the underworld is now complete. We see her transformation most clearly in the words of condemnation that she speaks against Dumuzi. As Inanna descended, she did not know the ways of the underworld. Upon her return, she cries against her callous husband with the same powerful death cry that was used upon her by her older sister. Inanna has now integrated the underworld powers of Ereshkigal. She has known death, been transformed by the food and water of life, and returned with the powers of the Great Below. Campbell observes that the two sisters together represent the two aspects of the one goddess, dark and light. Through her dark passage, Inanna "discovers and assimilates" her own unsuspected and opposite self.[20]

This story contains many familiar underworld journey motifs, including a threshold and gatekeeper, a descent through various layers or stages, the three-fold time measurement associated with death, a rebirth, and a return. Most significantly, it is also a story of transformation. Campbell notes that on such a journey, one must set aside pride, virtue, beauty, even life, and "bow or submit to the absolutely intolerable."[21] As Inanna descends, she is stripped of all disguises and adornments. She stands naked before the aspect of herself that lies deep and dark within. Confronted by this circumstance, she must succumb to the inevitable. She dies. Although the Anunnaki seem to foreshadow a judgment and punishment theme, they are not in fact weighing Inanna's guilt. Rather, their task is to pronounce the inevitable sentence for daring to penetrate to the innermost core. They have the eyes of death.

Here we might recall the primal belief that a new state cannot emerge without annihilation of the prior condition. The confrontation with her "dark side" requires that Inanna accomplish a radical transformation that can only come to pass by succumbing to the death of her former self. This is the foundational symbolic journey that will re-emerge in many different times and places. Passing into the depths of the "land of no return," the self is reduced to its most essential form. In the case of Inanna, the new self that emerges has integrated her dark aspects but has also been nourished by the water and food of life. Although the netherworld is the world of death, it finally comes to symbolize a realm of secret wisdom and transformation.

———————————————[the twice born]———————————————

Though the dark journey may be very familiar to some, it is not for everyone. In his classic *Varieties of Religious Experience,* the philosopher and psychologist, William James, breaks down human mystical experiences into two categories: the healthy minded and the sick soul. "Healthy minded" individuals are organically optimistic, disposed toward a cheerful nature and not inclined to linger over the darker aspects of the universe. Though they may, in fact, experience difficulties, they maintain a sense that the world is a good place and God is on their side. Sick souls, on the other hand, cannot help but experience the pain, evil, and suffering of the world, and through their realization of human helplessness in the face of such fear and pain, they develop a more profound awareness.

Those who navigate these dark waters and manage to emerge on the other side, James calls "the twice born." Emerging from the "dark night of the soul," one may experience a sense of deliverance and an awareness of the ultimate meaning of things. The world may appear more beautiful and more real, even though outward circumstances have not changed.

The underworld journey of myth symbolically illustrates this psychological death and rebirth and underscores the realization that human fear and suffering have always been with us. Many of us have "been through hell," and experienced a strong sense of all our carefully maintained ego structures dying away. We also recognize the experience of being stripped, as layer after layer of protective beliefs and behaviors are painfully removed. In the end, we must surrender to the death of what we have been. At this point, there is no awareness that return to the light is possible. Inanna could not see her tiny rescuers as they slipped through the gates and used compassion to win over the power of death. In the depths of the underworld, all we know is darkness. What then?

Before we move on to consider transformation and rebirth, we must pause again to note that some who descend never do find their way out. Many myths of the underworld describe individuals who are trapped in eternal suffering, condemned to endless, repetitive tasks.

Sisyphus was a greedy and deceitful king who became well known for his violence and his trickery. His greatest crime against the gods, however, was hubris, mortal arrogance, since he believed that his cleverness surpassed that of Zeus. The gods condemned him to Tartarus where he was made to push a huge boulder up a very steep hill. Before he could reach the top, the boulder would roll back down, so that he was condemned to perform this task for eternity.

This theme of endless torment extends to others who committed evil deeds, especially those who defied or betrayed the gods. Ixion was another Greek king whose evil deeds led him to be bound to a winged fiery wheel that would spin forever. The daughters of Danaus were required to carry jugs of water to fill a bottomless tub. Tantalus was required to stand in a pool of water under a fruit-bearing tree. Whenever he reached for the fruit or bent to drink the water, they moved just beyond his reach.

It is interesting to note that these punishments all reflect being stuck in a repetitive trap, eternally unable to transform or to move on. Likewise, there are those individuals in our ordinary lives that seem to be similarly stuck. Terrified of the ego disintegration required for true transformation, they remain trapped like deer in the headlights, afraid to move. They continually repeat the same patterns, afraid to risk the changes that might threaten the symbolic structures on which they have come to depend. This is not, however, any real comfort. The threat is always there, and escape remains impossible without letting go of the old ways of being. In this way, they become trapped in a hell of their own making.

Before moving on to darker underworld imagery, it is important to note that even if one succeeds in undergoing the necessary transformation and emerging from the netherworld, this is not the end of the journey. It is not even the end of the transformation. When Inanna condemns her husband, her actions and words indicate that she has integrated her dark nature. However, she does not immediately skip on home, all her tasks accomplished. The twice born often emerge from their underworld journey a little stunned by the light, just as a newborn emerges from the womb. Integrating the transformations that have taken place and realizing their import takes time and courage. Before Inanna's journey is complete, she will feel compassion for her errant husband and intervene on his behalf, as she integrates the forces of life and death with the power of love.

―――――――――――――――――――――[hell]――――――――――――――――――――

The English word for the land of the dead, hell, probably dates back to the Anglo-Saxon pagan period, but eventually this concept and terminology transfers into Christian theology. Most visions of hell associate punishment or suffering with specific sins committed in life. Though many depictions represent hell as a realm of fire, other traditions understand hell as cold, including some Christian mystic visions extending into the thirteenth century.

Condemnation of a soul to eternal suffering is typically associated with some form of judgment, such as that described as the weighing of souls in Egypt. Those who were taken by the devourer were first required to endure torture and then annihilated. These Egyptian images may have influenced medieval Christian perceptions of hell. Eventually the concept developed into a place where those who died in a state of mortal sin, without the benefit of God's gracious salvation, would suffer unending torture.

Although the concept of hell as a place of eternal punishment does not appear to be present in the Hebrew Bible, the term *Gehenna* appears in later rabbinic literature and in the New Testament as a metaphor for the final place of punishment for the wicked. Eventually, most Christian churches understood hell to be the final destiny of those who were judged and found wanting. These souls were doomed to eternal punishment and were to be separated from God after the general resurrection and last judgment. However, what constituted salvation from hell, whether doomed souls were mortal or immortal, and what happens to souls in hell after the last judgment vary somewhat from tradition to tradition.

This concept of eternal damnation has been often criticized for viewing a loving God as the cause of eternal suffering. However, Christian theology typically emphasizes that damnation to hell is a result of human rather than divine activity. For the most part, damnation is due to humanity's free actions in rejecting the command to love God and one's neighbor and turning only to self-serving interests. The problem, of course, is that it is difficult to understand what purpose, other than punishment, endless suffering could serve.

There is another Christian view. The ancient texts of the Apostles' Creed indicate that early Christians included in their confessions of faith a belief that after Jesus was crucified and died, he descended into hell, until on the third day, he rose from the dead.[22] This hell into which Jesus descended refers not to a place of eternal damnation but to Hades, the land of the dead. Jesus went into Hades for three days because the confession stated that he was raised from the dead—and that's where the dead were. Later Christian thinkers speculated at great length regarding what exactly Jesus did in the netherworld. However, the story of Jesus' descent into the underworld and return bears a striking resemblance to the mythical pattern of death and rebirth we have considered in various cultures. In order for the "new man" to rise, the old ego-self must die. Jesus dies to the flesh and three days later is raised in a new spiritual body. As we have seen, the place of this transition is the underworld.

——————————————[the bardo]————————————

Even when hell is understood as a place of suffering, however, it is not always understood as eternal. To find a more transitional understanding of hell, we must turn to so-called Eastern religious traditions, especially Buddhism. Buddhist texts teach that there are several realms of rebirth. After passing through the transitional state, the soul may be reborn as a human or an animal, a jealous god or a hungry ghost. At the extremes, there are several levels of heavens and hells. Because of the laws of karma, however, no realm of rebirth is permanent, including hell. Though suffering in the hell realms may last for eons, eventually the suffering soul will be reborn into a different realm.

One of the most complex and subtle portrayals of the passage after death is set out in the *Bardo Thosgrol Chenmo,* the Liberation through Hearing During the Intermediate State, informally known as the *Tibetan Book of the Dead.* This text was likely put into written form sometime around the eighth century CE and emerges from the tantric branch of the Mahayana Buddhist tradition in Tibet. Its primary function is to serve as a guide for the dying soul across the death threshold and through the intermediate state (the bardo) until one emerges into a future existence.[23] The text was to be read aloud as a guide to the dying in order to lead them to liberation. "Bardo" signifies the interval between death and rebirth, a transitional state often compared to a doorway or gate, through which one either passes into another realm of being or achieves liberation. The text describes the 49 days between death and rebirth and provides instructions along the way. Though rebirth into another realm of being is the most likely outcome, the teaching is actually designed to help the soul escape rebirth by recognizing that the various images it encounters are only one's own mental projections.

Although this concept of a transitional state after death may seem strange, there are experiences that confirm the power of this imagery. Sometimes, especially when nearing death, a person may seem to be passing beyond this realm, with one foot in this world and one foot in another. Perhaps aging individuals who are diagnosed with dementia have actually passed, at least partially, into the bardo. Though their bodily form is still here, and we may try to call them back, it seems clear that they are no longer really with us.[24]

The eighteen hell realms are not understood as places of punishment but rather as places into which one may be born as a direct result of accumulated karma. This distinction may be difficult to comprehend, but it is essential to understanding the nature of karmic transitions. We suffer because of our own hatred, anger and fear. Rather than being reward or punishment for past virtues and sins, karma is simply cause and effect. Our actions have consequences, now and in the future. These consequences collect in the form of karma. After the karma is used up, the soul will be reborn in another realm. This distinction is made more difficult for those accustomed to traditions based on reward and punishment, since descriptions of these hell realms are truly horrific. One text describes eight cold and eight hot hells into which a soul might be born, each filled with gruesome torments and torture. At the deepest levels, the soul's body might crack into pieces from cold or be boiled in oil or roasted in a burning oven.

A key to understanding the nature of these transitions is the Buddhist affirmation that whatever the existential experience, whether of heavens, hells, or regions in between, the ground of that experience is the mind of the one who experiences it. In the words of one Buddhist scholar, "We ourselves are responsible for our own happiness and misery. We create our own heavens. We create our own hells. We are the architects of our fate."[25]

From the Buddhist perspective, hell, like all other realms of existence, is mental, temporary and illusory, a state of mind bound up with karma from which escape depends in part upon recognition and acceptance. Transformation beyond the hell realms is certainly possible for all those who are willing to accept the realization that the experience of hell is one's own projection and responsibility. Hence, the way out of hell is associated with the death of the ego-self, a turning from prideful selfishness to a state of compassion. Even in a system based on transitions, the essential nature of transformation is emphasized. The hell realms are places of unbearable suffering. However, like all other forms of existence, souls are only in hell as long as they project themselves to be there. This is not meant to indicate that their suffering should be minimized. The terrors of the hell realm are not less horrifying for being projections. It is the work of the teaching to bring the soul to understand that the source of these terrors is within. If recognition is attained, fear is conquered and liberation is attained. If recognition cannot be attained, the horror becomes real, and the soul must wait out the eons of suffering until transition to another realm is accomplished.

In this way, the teachings of the *Tibetan Book of the Dead* involve not only the after death experience but the experience of death during life. In his introduction to the text, Graham Coleman stresses the importance of recognizing that our experiences are the result of the mental states that we ourselves have generated. Our own experience demonstrates that anger and fear alter our perceptions and affect our environment. "This is the cycle of experiencing the results of the mental state that we ourselves have generated, which can occur from moment to moment or … from lifetime to lifetime."

——————————{ chthonic residents }——————————

Though it looks like a typo, the term "chthonic" is actually derived from the Greek term "chthonios," meaning in, under or beneath the earth. For the ancient Greeks, the term came to refer to the deities or spirits of the underworld. Aside from those that are trapped in the underworld and those who succeed in completing the journey of metamorphosis, there are some who just belong there. For the mythic imagination, the chthonic realm is an essential source of power, and those that rule and dwell there have their own part to play.

rulers

Cultures worldwide not only describe an underworld or land of the dead but also feature some deity who rules over the dead. Their responsibilities vary, but typically part of their responsibility is to keep the dead where they belong. As in the story of Inanna, the underworld may have a female ruler, or the responsibility might be shared, as in the case of Persephone and Hades.

In Greek mythology, Hades (Pluto to the Romans) is the brother of Zeus and Poseidon. He drew lots with his brothers to see what regions they would rule. Zeus got the sky, Poseidon got the sea, and Hades got the "short straw." Among his attributes is the Helm of Darkness that renders him invisible when he wears it. He acquired his eventual consort and queen, Persephone, through trickery, but Hades is not depicted as an evil being. His role is to maintain balance, and he is typically portrayed as passive and unpitying but just. He does, however, fly into a rage whenever anyone attempts to leave his realm or to steal souls from him.

As noted above, the Greek queen of the underworld, Persephone, does not assume this role willingly. She is abducted by Hades from the upper world, but her mother, Demeter, manages to obtain her release. However, she must periodically return to Hades and function as queen of the underworld, receiving souls into the afterlife.

In the Hebrew Bible, satan is not an individual but a title (*ha-satan*, meaning "the accuser" or "the adversary") given to various beings, both human and divine, that challenge human faith. The classic example from the Hebrew Bible is in the book of Job, where the satan incites God to turn against Job in order to test his faith. However, some human enemies such as Hadam the Edomite are also referred to as ha-satan. There is some mention of ha-Satan as an individual in the Hebrew Apocrypha, the Tal-mud, and other Jewish sources, typically as an agent of God who is as-signed the task of tempting people into sin. This is probably the source of the traditional view that the serpent who tempts Eve to eat the forbidden fruit is actually Satan, although the story itself makes no such reference.

The Greeks translated this term into diabolos ("slanderer") from which the term "devil" in the New Testament is derived. The concept of Satan develops within Christianity over time, including the eventual association of Satan with Lucifer, the fallen "son of the dawn" (Isaiah 14:12). Various depictions of Satan represent him as a serpent, a dragon, or a winged monster.

Eventually, Christians came to understand Satan as an angel who re-belled against God and who seeks to turn humanity away from obedi-ence to God. Initially, Satan was the highest of the angels, but in his pride he would not bow down to God but sought to rule heaven himself. This understanding of Satan is not specifically portrayed in scripture but is in-ferred from certain passages in Ezekiel and Isaiah. In the book of Revela-tions, Satan is a dragon-monster who will be cast out of heaven to wage war against believers until he, along with many others, will be cast into the Lake of Fire to suffer for all eternity.

The origin of the concept that Satan rules over a realm of eternal pun-ishment is unclear. The books of Matthew and Revelations suggest that Satan will eventually be cast into hell, and other texts suggest that he is the god of the earthly realm. Although a few Biblical texts do address a realm of the wicked or a place of torment, there is no indication that Satan rules there.

Many other cultures also depict a supernatural being that personifies evil and struggles with the divine over the souls of humans. In Islam, for example, God created Iblis out of smokeless fire, while man was created out of clay. Believing himself to be superior because of his origins, Iblis refused to pay homage to Adam and was expelled by God. Whether impas-sive judges or evil tempters, however, the rulers of the underworld guard their resident souls well, and escape without transformation is impossible.

monsters

Some ancient mapmakers illustrated the uncharted areas of the ocean with images of dragons and sea serpents, sometimes adding the phrase, "Here there be monsters." Cross the boundary that divides the ordered and civ-ilized realms from chaotic wilderness, and you find yourself in strange company. In his reflection on monsters in religion, Timothy Beal observes that all monsters, from those depicted on ancient maps to representations in contemporary pop culture, "stand on and for the threshold between world and abyss."[26]

> They are personification of that which is in the world but not of it, appearing on the ambiguous edges of the conceptual landscape, where the right order of things touches on a wholly other chaos, where inside and outside, self and other intertwine.[27]

Whether demons, gods, or something in between, monsters bring on an experience, akin to religious experience, of being "on the edge of certainty and security," both drawn and repulsed by mysterious power. The monstrous is "an embodiment of overwhelming and chaotic excess, a too-muchness that brings on a vertigo-like sense of fear and desire; standing on the threshold of an unfathomable abyss."[28]

The denizens of the deep come in many forms, and we cannot include them all here, but a few examples will illustrate the hidden significance of the truly monstrous. Though not all of them dwell in the underworld, they all belong in one way or another to the chthonic realm.

Interestingly, the Biblical monsters of the sea quite specifically belong to God. Tales of the *tannin* (sea monsters) and the monsters Yam, Leviathan and other water serpent demons were probably part of Near Eastern mythology as far back as the third millennium BCE, and Hebrew monsters were probably close equivalents to Ugaritic monster gods with very similar names. In Psalm 104, however, Leviathan is specifically named as one of God's creations. Here Leviathan is imagined as "a frolicsome creature of divine delight."[29] This psalm, a joyous celebration of God's creation, brings to mind that the first creatures specifically named in Genesis as God's creations are monsters: "So God created the great sea monsters [*tanninim*] and every living creature that moves, of every kind, with which the waters swarm ..." (Genesis 1:21).

Psalm 74, a psalm of lament, depicts a very different relationship between God and his sea monster. Though this psalm also underscores God's supreme creative power, here God defeats and crushes Leviathan, along with all the other sea monsters, as part of the task of fixing the earth's boundaries. Job 41 describes Leviathan in vivid detail, complete with fearsome teeth, eyes like rays of dawn, a mouth that shoots sparks and flame, and breath that sets coals ablaze. Certainly, this is a creature only God can handle.

Monsters associated with water and myths related to them appear all over the world. The Scots tell of ashrays, translucent water creatures that are completely nocturnal, because they melt into water when exposed to the sun. In aboriginal Australia, the bunyip lurked in swamps and water holes and used humans as a food source, especially women. Scandinavian waters were filled with demons and spirits.

Returning to Biblical mythology, Behemoth is the land equivalent of Leviathan, and he also appears in the book of Job to demonstrate the pointlessness of questioning God. Only God could create such power, and only God can tame or capture it. Beal points out that this description of Behemoth is certainly intended to inspire "more dread than wonder at God's ways in the world."[30]

In later Jewish writing, Behemoth was understood to live in an invisible desert east of Eden, while Leviathan lives in the Abyss. By the second century CE, Behemoth is the primal unconquerable monster of the land, and Leviathan is the primal monster of the seas. Tannin and Rahab are related monsters in Jewish folklore, especially associated with the Red Sea. They are variously understood as sea-demons, serpents and dragons. As visions of hell become more and more associated with evil and punishment, Leviathan becomes one of the seven princes of hell, serving as its gatekeeper.

Mention has already been made of Cerberus, the three-headed guard hound of hell. Cerberus actually comes from an interesting family, since his parents are a hybrid serpent-woman and Typhon, the fire breathing giant, and his siblings include the Hydra, the Sphinx and the Chimera, among others. He is also said to have a mane of live serpents and a snake's tail.

One trait these monsters seem to have in common is an association with snakes or serpents. The serpent is one of the oldest and most widespread mythic symbols, and rituals associated with it can be traced to some of the most ancient cultures. It would be difficult to come up with another creature that has such a complex set of symbolic references, but certain traits and associations appear very frequently. In particular, the snake has been associated with fertility, wisdom, and transformation, as well as deceitfulness, trickery, and death. Another ubiquitous image is the serpent biting its own tail (most commonly known by the Greek term of Ourobouros), representing the totality of existence or the unity of the cosmos as well as the eternal circle of life.

Some of these associations probably come from the serpent's physical characteristics. The forked tongue, pointing in different directions, may symbolize deceitful speech or trickery. Defensive or aggressive behavior could be associated with protection, while the serpent's venom not only symbolizes poison but also medicine, wisdom and divine intoxication. The most obvious symbolic characteristic is, of course, the shedding of skin, representing transformation and even rebirth. Other related mythical creatures share some or all of these characteristics, including the Hydra, the Basilisk, the Hindu nagas, and various dragons.

Though it is impossible to cover all the monstrous creatures of chaos, we must at least make note of those that swallow us whole. Of course, Jonah comes first to mind, though many other myths feature gods and heroes being swallowed by monsters. The dynamics between God and Jonah in this story are complicated, but the plot is quite simple. Jonah, having disobeyed God, tries to run away by ship. God calls up a storm, and the sailors toss Jonah overboard to appease God. A great fish immediately swallows Jonah, and he spends three days and three nights languishing in the fish's belly. Jonah repents and prays for mercy, God speaks to the fish, and the fish vomits him out safely onto dry land. Jonah goes on to become a powerful prophet for the Lord.

Simple though this story might be, the symbolic elements are so powerful that this ancient imagery has carried forward into contemporary culture. A "belly of the whale" experience in common parlance involves entering into deep reflection prior to facing a very difficult task. One then emerges from this dormant state with greater courage, clarity and determination. The three-day duration of Job's sojourn in the deep is, of course, no accident. Whether we view the belly of the whale as the subconscious, the abyss, or the underworld, it is the realm of transformation in which the old being is swallowed whole and the new being emerges.

Not all heroes pass through hell, and not all those who enter hell ever return. This imagery of an underworld descent and return does, however, provide us with a symbolic alternative that may prove useful when our lives seem to be falling apart. In contemporary culture, a great premium is placed on maintaining order. We diligently seek to "keep it together," even when we feel as if we are going to pieces. With Inanna, we put on our symbols of authority and do what we can to avoid the abyss. The poet, Yeats, was probably right, however, that the center will not hold. Things really do fall apart. Sometimes we feel that our most cherished social and psychological structures are being stripped away. As we endure these "little deaths," it may seem as if we are slipping into the dark.

The mythic underworld journey suggests that, rather than indicating some kind of psychic failure, this coming apart may be necessary so that a new being can emerge. As we descend, the layers of protection are stripped away and the old ego structures die. At the deepest levels of this descent, there is a tremendous release of transformative energy. Finally, over time, a new self comes together and emerges, born from the ashes and returning to a world that can now be understood in a new way.

[chapter] **5**

RENEWAL, RESURRECTION, AND RETURN

Home is this season of winter light,

the heartbeat of seeds deepening,

a gathering of seven yellow leaves.

This is my promise.

Everlasting journey

and the lights of home.

Tessier

Just outside the village, a traveler slowly approaches. He is dusty and trav-el-worn, walking with a trace of a limp. As he comes closer, he leaves the road and skirts the village, quietly gazing at the houses and fields. Some-thing about him looks familiar, but the villagers can't quite place him. He looks as if he has come a long way. Finally, he approaches a small house on the other side of town, walks up the path, and lowers his traveling pack from his shoulders. Turning away, one of the villagers says to another, "Looks like he's been through hell." The hero has returned.

Since the mythic pattern is cyclical, the hero's journey ends where it began, at home. However, as Thomas Wolfe made clear, one can never tru-ly go home again, because the old forms and systems of things will never be the same. Returning heroes are not the same as the ones who departed; their homes are not the same as the ones they left. Some will eventually greet them with joy and fond memories while others will react to them with suspicion. As Campbell notes, "The returning hero, to complete his (sic) adventure, must survive the impact of the world."[1]

What would seem to be the most joyous aspect of the hero's adven-ture, the return home, actually represents another extraordinary challenge, the "final crisis of the round."[2] The hero must now re-cross the threshold between the mythic realm and the ordinary world, returning to "the long forgotten atmosphere where men who are fractions imagine themselves to be complete."[3]

This return is of particular significance because heroes do not return from mythic journeys empty handed. They bear with them great gifts with the power to benefit all humanity, if only they can bring others to comprehend these boons. In this last great feat, the hero must "confront society with his ego-shattering, life-redeeming elixir, and take the return blow of reasonable queries, hard resentment, and good people at a loss to comprehend."[4]

But we are a bit ahead of ourselves. How does the hero come to be back at the beginning? What is the journey from the depths of darkness to this place? As we have seen, ascent from the chaotic realms can only be achieved through metamorphosis, so the hero who ascends is always a new being. We can begin to explore this last phase of the hero's journey, therefore, by considering this renewal or rebirth in greater depth.

[rebirth]

Numerous narratives describe this transition, and we have already dis-cussed several of them. At the outset, however, it is important to stress again that these ancient stories are dynamic. If there is an "original" version, we are very unlikely to discover it. Rather than seeking the "true" version, we can be assured that every version contains powerful symbols that have influenced past cultures and carry their multivalent meanings into the present and the future.

[osiris]

One rebirth narrative that may lend us some insight is that of Osiris. As mentioned above, Osiris is believed by many scholars to be one of the earliest symbolic manifestations of the dying and rising gods, initially associated with both fertility and death. However, over time his cult became primarily concerned with his role as a savior deity and as the primary ruler over "those who are not," the dead in *Duat.*

There are multiple versions of his death and resurrection narrative, but a general summary of events serves to illustrate his role in the rebirth narrative. Osiris and his sister-wife, Isis, were children of the goddess Nut. They came to rule over all Egypt and were envied and hated by their brother, Seth, lord of evil. Through trickery, Seth killed Osiris and eventually dismembered him. Isis managed to recover all the parts of her divine husband's body (with the exception of his phallus that had been eaten by fishes). She constructed a new phallus of gold and, with the help of Nut, succeeded in resurrecting him. In some accounts she is said to have transformed herself into a great bird (the kite) and used her wings to breathe life back into him, conceiving her son Horus in the process.

Whether this was a bodily or a spiritual resurrection (or a resurrection at all) has been much debated, but various versions of the myth agree that Osiris was brought to life in order to die again, this time with the proper burial ceremonies, so that he could pass into the blessed land to become king of the underworld and lord of the dead. His fertility and funerary aspects combined to underscore his role as a primary deity of resurrection. As his cult developed, the dead were identified with Osiris, traveling with him through the difficult underworld passage. Initially, only dead kings merited this identification. The oldest Osiris litany in the Pyramid Texts (Utterance 219) states "he [Osiris] lives, this king lives: he [Osiris] is not dead, this king is not dead." Thus the continuing afterlife of the king was based on the continued life of Osiris.[5] With the First Intermediate Period (2181-2055 BCE), a certain "democratization of the underworld" took place in Egyptian beliefs, and it became possible for any deceased person to assume the guise of Osiris and achieve life after death.

The Egyptian texts known as the *Book of Going Forth by Day,* now commonly referred to as the Egyptian *Book of the Dead,* were believed to provide guidance to accomplish this journey. Their purpose was to assist the deceased in leaving the tomb and attaining a satisfactory afterlife. There is no single or canonical form of these texts, but various collections of religious and magical material were in use from about 1550 BCE to around 50 BCE. Some spells were drawn from older works and may date as far back as the third millennium BCE. Typically, they were written in hieroglyphic or hieratic script on a papyrus scroll, often illustrated with vignettes depicting the deceased on the journey into the afterlife, and placed in the coffin or burial chamber of the deceased.

The ancient *Papyrus of Ani* is probably the best surviving example, written and illustrated around 1250 BCE by unknown scribes and artists. In the introductory hymn of praise to Osiris, he is called King of Kings, Lord of Lords, and Ruler of Rulers as well as King of Eternity and Lord of Everlasting. Another text entitled the *Theban Recension* consists of chapters that do not appear in the Papyrus of Ani. Chapter 64 of that text, entitled "Chapter of knowing all the chapters of going forth by day in a single chapter," is often considered to be a summary of all the various hymns and spells. Though the ancient language is obscure, reverence for Osiris and his association with death and rebirth seem clear:

> He says: Yesterday, which is pregnant with the one who shall give birth to himself at another time, belongs to me. I am the one secret of Ba-spirit who made the gods and gives offerings to the Duat gods of the West of the sky … I am he and he is I.
>
> …
>
> I know the depths and I know your name. You have made the portions of the blessed dead…
>
> …
>
> Gather me together, gather me together, that I may soar up and alight upon land. My eye races thereby in my footsteps. I am one who gave birth to myself yesterday, one who created my own name.[6]

Although crucial to achieving an afterlife, these texts were not sufficient to assure success. Acquiring a good afterlife also required considerable effort during life. One needed a tomb, a large number of burial objects, and the preservation of one's body and one's name in order to reach the hoped-for fields of paradise. Those who attained a good afterlife wished to be in the company of Osiris and to travel in the bark of the solar deity, Re.

The Field of Rushes and the Field of Offerings were in many respects identical to the living world. A river flowed through them, fields on either bank produced food, and the sun traveled through the sky, passing through the underworld while the upper world experienced night. The deceased hoped to enjoy the sunlight, feast in paradisiacal fields of offerings, and be cared for by goddesses. The location of the realms of the dead varied greatly from text to text, however, and descriptions were by no means limited to underworld geography. For example, some tomb inscriptions refer to the starry heavens or the "beautiful west" (the mountains west of the Nile where the sun sets) as the land of the dead.

————————[other myths of rebirth]————————

Death and rebirth imagery has also been associated with Tammuz, the Babylonian god of food and vegetation. Tammuz is in many ways the equivalent of Dumuzi, and his consort, Ishtar, is the counterpart to the Sumerian goddess, Inanna. He is connected with agriculture and livestock as well as wild animals, and various cults conducted ritual mourning for him at the time of the summer solstice. According to one tradition, all vegetation dies along with Tammuz, but Ishtar raises him up from the underworld in the spring, and life returns to the world. Several scholars add Tammuz to the list of vegetation deities who are also associated with death and rebirth.

In addition to Osiris, Tammuz, and the Inanna and Persephone accounts described in previous chapters, some form of rebirth or resurrection has been attributed to Adonis, Attis, Asclepius, Orpheus, Odin and Dionysus, among others. In Sir James Frazer's monumental study, *The Golden Bough,* he considers a number of these accounts. Later scholarship has challenged many of his interpretations, and we will probably never completely untangle the complexities that arise regarding the names, titles, and narratives attributed to these heroes and deities. Regardless of what stories preceded others and what deities were actually cognates or derivatives of other deities, the symbolism of rebirth and renewal remains. Many scholars associate the dying-and-rising imagery in these traditions with natural cycles such as the "death and rebirth" of vegetation or the waning and waxing of the moon.

In some of these accounts, the hero is reborn in some non-human form. Attis, for example, is born from Nana, a virgin who conceives by placing a ripe almond (or a pomegranate) in her bosom. Though there are conflicting accounts of his death, Attis is reborn as an evergreen pine. In other narratives, gods or heroes are "twice born," because they are preserved from destruction and born again by the act of a deity. In one account, Zeus fell in love with a mortal princess, Semele. Dionysus was conceived from their union, but jealous Hera used trickery to bring about his mother's death while he was still in the womb. Zeus then rescued Dionysus from Semele's womb and sewed the fetus into his own thigh where it gestated until birth. This very odd form of surrogacy is the reason why Dionysus is called the "twice born."

Whoever the associated deities may have been, Adonis or Osiris, Demeter or Dionysus, ancient mystery cults devoted to them offered initiates secret knowledge and rebirth through participation in their power. The best known of these are undoubtedly the Eleusinian mysteries carried out by the cult of Demeter and Persephone at Eleusis. Although the details of these rituals are obscure, it is clear that initiates hoped through participation in them to obtain blessings (whether spiritual or material) in the afterlife. Though most of these cults are associated with ancient Greece and Rome, there are equivalents in other cultures and religions.

───────────────[resurrection]───────────────

The literal return to life of the biologically dead is a very specific form of rebirth. One significant aspect of this transformation is that the resurrected one is often a mortal who is thereby typically rendered immortal, although there are exceptions. When the prophets Elijah and Elisha raised the dead, there is no account that the resurrected ones become immortal. Jesus raised Lazarus and others from the dead, but it is assumed that they died a second time.

Many of the Greek accounts describe a transformation from mortal to immortal. Zeus killed Asclepius with a thunderbolt but placed him in the stars as the constellation Ophiuchus (the serpent bearer). He became known as the Greek god of medicine and healing. Heracles, son of Zeus and the mortal Alcmena, is significant as a man born of mortal woman who becomes a god after his death. As Heracles lay upon his funeral pyre and the flames grew, a great cloud appeared, a bolt of lightening struck, and the body of Heracles disappeared. He was made immortal and taken up to Mount Olympus to live among the gods. Various other Greek heroes were sometimes considered to have obtained immortality.

These transformations emphasized the continuance of the body and its reunion with the soul, as contrasted with those who existed only as disembodied and dead souls. Some later Greek philosophers, however, specifically denied the possibility of physical immortality, holding that the soul could transcend death, but decayed flesh could not be restored. Greek philosophy included other theoretical positions regarding life after death, including the transmigration of souls and even the return of the soul to life in the physical world, though not necessarily in human form.

Odin (Wotan in the Germanic tradition) is king and father of the gods in Norse mythology. His multidimensional story underscores certain resurrection themes. Ancient stories pertaining to him, along with other Norse mythology, are set out in the Icelandic Eddas. A god of warriors and battle, he was also known by over 200 other names. Along with his many associations with battle and violence, Odin was associated with the land of the dead, wisdom, magic, poetry, and deception. In fact, his names and characteristics are so numerous and complex that it is quite impossible to categorize him. Odin's name literally means frenzy, and he is most profoundly associated with states and conditions (like the battlefield or sexual ecstasy) that are out of control.

Among the stories associated with him, the most well-known have to do with his desire for wisdom and secret knowledge. In one account, he cast one of his eyes into Mimir's well in return for a drink of its wisdom. He also voluntarily sacrificed himself by hanging on the cosmic tree, *Yggdrasil,* for nine days and nights without food and water in order to achieve initiation into secret wisdom. This spiritual death and resurrection by magic lifted him above all others in wisdom. In some accounts, he was pierced by a spear during this ordeal, and there is prehistoric evidence of human and animal sacrifices to Odin that were hung on trees, often pierced by spears.

Another interesting aspect of Odin's mythology is the concept of Ragnarok, a future cosmic battle when the fate of the gods will be determined. Through his expanded wisdom, Odin could see into the future and understood what would occur during these end times. Many of the great gods would die, including Odin, killed by a monstrous wolf, and natural disasters and flooding would bring about the total immersion of the world in water. Afterward, a new world would emerge from the waters, the surviving and reborn gods would meet again, and the world would be repopulated.

[jesus]

The imagery of these ancient stories sometimes calls to mind what is probably the most familiar resurrection story of all time—that of Jesus. Many of the attributes associated with the Jesus story (virgin birth, birth marked by a star, death by hanging on a tree, three days between death and rebirth, etc.) can also be found in other ancient stories. Some scholars, mainly based on Sir James Frazer's parallels in *The Golden Bough,* suggest not only that there was widespread worship of a dying and rising god in the ancient world but also that the Christian resurrection story is a myth based on that ancient prototype. A lively debate continues regarding the impact of these early stories, but there is no doubt that many stories of rebirth and perhaps even of bodily resurrection preceded the Christian account.

Although the tradition of Jesus' resurrection is celebrated in many cultures across the globe, the early accounts of events surrounding the death, burial, and resurrection of Jesus varied. All four gospels testify that Jesus was crucified and that Joseph of Arimathea asked Pilate for his body, which was then wrapped in linen cloth and laid in a tomb according to Mosaic law. Though the gospels do not contain any reference to a sojourn in the afterworld before his resurrection, the Book of Revelations contains a passage in which Jesus says, "Do not be afraid; I am the first and the last, and the living one. I was dead, and see, I am alive for ever and ever; and I have the keys of Death and of Hades" (Rev. 1:17-18). This passage, together with one verse in 1 Peter, serves as the basis for the statement in the Apostle's Creed that Jesus descended into Hades after death.

There are, of course, no accounts of the actual resurrection event. The belief that Jesus rose from the dead emerged from accounts indicating that his tomb was found empty and the testimony of various individuals claiming to have seen him after death. Although the day of Jesus' crucifixion is unclear, various traditions hold that Jesus was dead for three days before rising from the dead. Others say that he was resurrected on the third day. The only point upon which all four gospels agree is that various women went to visit the tomb about sunrise on the first day of the week and found it empty. They also concur that the risen Christ chose to appear to a woman (or women) and instructed her (or them) to proclaim his resurrection to the apostles. Unlike the apostles, the women recognized him.

There are several accounts of Jesus' appearance after death in the gospels and in the writings of Paul. In one account, Jesus meets two of his disciples on the road to Emmaus, but they fail to recognize him. Later, however, as they are sharing a meal, their eyes are opened, and they know him. In other accounts, he appears to the disciples on a mountaintop in the Galilee or in an upper room. John records another appearance to the disciples during which Thomas doubts his identity until Jesus invites him to put his fingers into the wounds. Luke describes an event forty days after the resurrection when Jesus ascends into heaven. Paul of Tarsus also reported a vision of the risen Jesus as he was traveling the road to Damascus. In his writings, Paul also lists appearances of the resurrected Jesus to several men, but does not describe them.

For Christians, of course, Jesus is the only incarnation of the one God, and this resurrection occurred only once, to one being. The mystical drama of the resurrection implies both personal and cosmic regeneration through re-actualizing Christ's birth, death, and resurrection.[7]

Perhaps no event in religious history has been so much debated. Scholars and theologians disagree about everything from the date of his death to his after-death appearances to whether he actually rose from the dead. Reports of his appearances after death have even been attributed to some form of hallucination or ecstatic experience. From the perspective of the myth, however, the truth of the story lies in its symbolic meaning and cannot be undone by history. He died suffering. He traveled to the underworld and remained with the dead for three days. He arose, so transformed that those who saw him did not recognize him. He died for the benefit of all humanity, and his return from death transformed the world.

Especially given the extraordinary drama of the event, mythic accounts of resurrection tend to be rather quiet. There are no blaring trumpets or brilliant rays of light in the ancient stories. Old friends meet on the road and share a meal. A beloved goddess, once dead, calls out to her devoted follower who falls weeping at her feet. A strange old man appears in the middle of a field. When one who has died returns to life, the emotions of mixed grief and joy take place deep in the private places of the heart. Interestingly, the risen one does not call for revenge or encourage followers to take up arms. Rather, the message throughout these narratives is fairly consistent—a call for courage, peace, and faith, along with an ongoing promise of guidance and support from the risen one.

———————[symbols of rebirth and renewal]———————

It should not come as a shock that resurrection symbols are intimately associated with fertility and transformation symbols. Whether the focus is on the Great Goddess or Jesus, we recognize the fecund powers that bring life back into the world, and we respond to the symbols that represent them. Aside from the death and rebirth of deities and heroes, mythical imagery represents this symbolism in myriad forms.

A prominent example, evident in many cultures from China to Mexico, is the phoenix. This mythical bird is typically associated with the sun and its daily journey from birth to death, only to be born again with the next sunrise. It is therefore also a symbol of rebirth, immortality, and renewal. Even the name of the city of Phoenix maintains this association with rebirth, since the city was built on the ruins of the ancient Hohokam civilization.

Names and physical descriptions vary from culture to culture, although the plumage of this fire spirit is always colorful, often with a tail of gold or scarlet. It is said to have a long life cycle, typically from 500 to 1,000 years (though some accounts extend its life as far as 12,994 years). At the end of this period, the phoenix builds a nest (often of herbs and spices) and then usually ignites itself. In some traditions, the same bird is resurrected from the ashes, while in others a new phoenix or phoenix egg arises, born again to repeat the process. Although most stories of the phoenix describe it as a benevolent creature, it could also sometimes be dangerous.

Scholars and poets from Ovid to St. Clement have written about the phoenix, and birds ranging from the heron to the flamingo have been associated with it. The word "phoenix" probably derives from the Greek word for the color crimson, also meaning palm tree.

One ancient version is the Egyptian benu bird, described in the *Egyptian Book of the Dead* and other texts. Its name was probably derived from the term "weben," meaning to "rise" or "shine." This bird was one of the sacred images of Heliopolis, and was likely the prototype for the Greek phoenix. Later versions of the myth describe the phoenix's flight from Arabia to the temple of the sun at Heliopolis. The benu was also associated with Atum, Re and Osiris and with the annual flooding of the Nile. One tradition indicates that the benu flew over the waters of Nun at the creation, and the cry of the sacred bird marked the beginning of time. Like the sun god, the benu was thought to be "self-created," appearing under the rising sun and shining over the world from a sacred tree at Heliopolis where the great bird renewed itself. Chapter 83 of the *Egyptian Book of the Dead* contains a spell for turning the deceased into a benu-bird. There are also strong links between the benu bird and the benben stone at Heliopolis, a sacred stone that symbolized the primeval mound where the first acts of creation took place.

It may also have been this Egyptian version that influenced inclusion of the phoenix in Christian bestiaries, volumes from the Middle Ages describing animals and other natural entities. The descriptions and illustrations in these texts also typically included moral lessons, often connecting the behavior of animals to religious values and beliefs. One of the best known, the Aberdeen Bestiary, claims that the phoenix represents the resurrection of the righteous who gather the aromatic plants of virtue and prepare themselves for the renewal that will follow death. Therefore, the phoenix offers proof of the resurrection to ordinary people through the workings of nature.

Chinese and Japanese accounts of the phoenix vary greatly from those associated with the Greek and Arabic traditions, but they also maintain a certain association with dying and rising imagery. This mythical bird (Feng Huang in China, Hou-ou in Japan) was also associated with fire and with the sun. It appeared very rarely, only to indicate the beginning of a new peaceful and prosperous era, and it disappeared at times of disharmony, returning to celestial realms to await a new era. In both China and Japan, where the empress historically had enormous power in certain dynasties, the phoenix was the symbol of the empress, while the dragon represented the emperor. Chinese images of the phoenix can be traced back well over 7,000 years.

Although countless images express the theme of rebirth, we will limit our discussion to one additional image: the lotus. As with the benu bird, Egyptian mythology also associated the lotus (*sesen*) with the sun, creation and rebirth. Since the lotus blossom closes at night, sinks below the surface of the water, and then rises and opens with the light, some creation myths depicted a golden lotus emerging out of watery chaos at the beginning of time. This luminous bloom brought both light and perfume to the world. It was known as "the redolent flower" and "the soul of Re," and some traditions held that the sun god hid inside its bloom to be revealed when the lotus opened its blossom. Atum and Re were depicted as emerging from a lotus, and the flower was also associated with the cult of Osiris. As with the benu bird, the *Book of the Dead* has a spell that can be used for the dead to transform into a lotus flower. The blue lotus was the symbol of the Egyptian god, Nefertum, a solar deity linked to various creation stories. The lotus also became the symbol for Upper Egypt and was included in depictions of rulers from that region. Thus, imagery of the sun, rebirth, and the origin of things was united with the reality of political events.[8]

However, the symbol of the lotus (Sanskrit: *padma*) is probably most commonly associated with Hindu and Buddhist mythology. Many Hindu deities are portrayed as sitting or lying upon a lotus, and one Hindu creation story relates that Brahma, the Hindu creator god, was self-born from a lotus flower that grew from the navel of Vishnu at the beginning of the universe. Since the lotus is rooted in the mud but floats in pristine beauty on the surface of the water, it also serves as a symbol of non-attachment. While the lotus is associated with creation in Buddhism, it is primarily a symbol of purification and enlightenment. The six syllable mantra *om mane padme hum* is typically translated "The jewel is in the lotus" and is strongly associated with the bodhisattva Avalokitesvara and the Dalai Lama. Like the phoenix and lotus imagery, symbolic representation of rebirth takes on a different focus in Hindu and Buddhist traditions.

———————————————{ the karmic cycle }———————————————

While many mythologies symbolize our human longing for rebirth and everlasting life, we cannot comprehensively discuss these motifs without taking note of traditions that view such longings from a very different perspective—as something that must ultimately be transcended. For the traditions discussed above, rebirth in a new body may be viewed as a miracle. For some other traditions, it is just what happens until one develops sufficient wisdom to escape.

Though the term "reincarnation" is probably most familiar, the concept that the soul or spirit is reborn in a new form has historically been understood and named in various ways. As with so many concepts represented by ancient symbols and narratives, this topic is far too complex to cover in any detail. A discussion of some basic concepts can, however, illustrate the significance of this very different understanding of rebirth.

To reduce the very complex subject of reincarnation to its most basic form, when one dies, though one's body passes away, something of oneself is reborn. Though this view of life after death is most commonly associated in contemporary culture with the religions emerging from India, there is historical evidence of this view among Greek philosophers, Druids, and some early Jewish and Christian sects. There are so many technical distinctions regarding such issues as the nature of the self or soul, the workings of karma, and the path to enlightenment that several complex schools of philosophy have developed around these issues. Here, however, we are concerned not with technical definitions and concepts but with the images and stories that bring these ideas about rebirth to life.

At first it may seem that this understanding of rebirth takes us far off the path of the hero's journey, but in fact it may be only the length of the journey (and perhaps the "final" destination) that differs very much. Here, too, we find departure and return, encounters with trials and obstacles, and the cycle of death, transformation, and rebirth.

Even those who will eventually attain the highest levels of enlightenment must first experience *samara* (the seemingly endless karmic cycle of life, death, and rebirth). Stories of the various incarnations of the Buddha are particularly helpful in revealing the cosmic significance of this path. The *Jataka* is an ancient collection of stories about the Buddha's life experiences before his last human incarnation. Among these are tales of the Buddha's lives in the form of animals. These tales, often translated in forms suitable for children, are among the most moving narratives to be found in the vast literature of Buddhist texts.

The story of the selfless hare, for example, reveals much about the character of the Buddha. Once again, the narrative is a bit too long to be set out in full, so we must resort to a synopsis.

A monkey, an otter, a jackal, and a hare resolved to practice charity on the day of the full moon. When an old man begged for food, the monkey offered mangoes it had gathered from the trees, and the otter offered the fish he had collected. The jackal had taken a lizard and a pot of milk-curd that someone else had abandoned, and he offered that to the old man. The hare only knew how to gather grass and felt that this would not be a suitable offering. Instead, the hare threw himself into the fire, offering his own body. The old man then revealed himself to be Sakra, king of the devas, and he caused the fire to become cold so that the hare would not be burned. Touched by the hare's virtue, he drew the likeness of the hare on the moon for all to see.

Though more fable than myth, this tale goes far beyond a mere lesson about the value of charity. The hare offers his body with great joy, aware of the karmic benefits that will accrue to the whole world from his act of compassion. Perhaps even more significantly, he is glad in his heart to make the sacrifice, because the old man will have something to eat.

In these traditions, acts of compassion are heroic deeds, regardless of the nature of the act itself. What is most significant is not the act or even the consequences of the act but the motivation or will of the doer. Another Buddha incarnation narrative from a Mahayana sutra illustrates this point. In one of his human lives, the Buddha was captain of a ship carrying 500 bodhisattvas disguised as merchants. There was also a thief on board who planned to kill all the passengers and steal the ship's cargo. Knowing the heart of the thief and realizing what he planned to do, the Buddha was aware of the eons of torment the thief would suffer for his murderous deed. Out of compassion, the Buddha killed the thief, realizing that he would have to bear hellish torment himself for committing a murder, but his suffering would be much less than the thief would have to endure if he carried through with his plan. It is important to stress that the Buddha's compassion was not for the bodhisattvas, who would not suffer karmic injury, but for the thief. By his act, the Buddha literally took the sin of murder upon himself.

Perhaps the relationship between reincarnation and the hero's journey can best be demonstrated by considering two very special sorts of beings: the Hindu avatar and the Buddhist bodhisattva. For these beings, rebirth itself is a form of compassionate sacrifice.

The concept of the avatar in Vaishnava Hinduism is similar in some ways to the Christian view. In both traditions, a divine being assumes human bodily form on earth in order to benefit or save humanity. An avatar (from the Sanskrit word for "descent") is a deity who intentionally descends to earth in bodily form during times of moral and social decline in order to restore balance between good and evil. This term is most commonly applied to Vishnu, whose many appearances as an avatar, both animal and human, are variously listed in several ancient texts. Among his best-known manifestations are the deities Krishna and Rama. However, some Hindus suggest that divine beings such as Buddha and Jesus were also avatars of Vishnu.

The avatar's purpose for incarnating on earth is set out in the very popular Hindu text, the *Bhagavad Gita,* here manifested as Krishna:

> Whenever dharma [righteousness] declines and the purpose of life
> is forgotten, I manifest myself on earth. I am born into every age to
> protect the good, to destroy evil, and to reestablish dharma.
> (Bhagavad Gita: 4.7–8)[9]

Unlike the Chinese phoenix bird that disappears in times of disorder and unrest and reappears as a sign of a new and more harmonious age, Vishnu's avatars appear on earth in order to restore righteousness.

A different but somewhat related concept is that of the Buddhist bodhisattva. The various branches of Buddhism understand the nature of the bodhisattva somewhat differently. Though the term means something like "enlightenment-being," the principal trait of the bodhisattva is compassion. Most commonly, the bodhisattva is understood as a realized being, capable of liberation from samsara, who vows instead to renounce the ultimate state in favor of helping others along the path to enlightenment until all beings have attained it.

Among the most revered of all bodhisattvas is Avalokitesvara, said to embody the compassion of all the Buddhas. One of his Sanskrit names, Padmapani, means holder of the lotus. This being, also represented in female form as Kwan Yin, hears the cries of all sentient beings and strives endlessly to alleviate their suffering. In Tibetan Buddhism, the Dalai Lama (now in his 14th incarnation) is considered to be the primary earthly manifestation of the great bodhisattva (known in Tibet as *Chenrezig*).

Tara, a female bodhisattva known as the mother of liberation, is considered to be a female manifestation of Avalokitesvara. She is known as a goddess of compassion and action who appears in order to alleviate suffering. When Avalokitesvara was weeping out of compassion for the suffering on earth, his tear fell to the ground to become a lake. Out of this lake there emerged a lotus that opened to reveal the goddess. In another story, Tara emerges directly from the heart of Avalokitesvara. One interesting aspect of Tara is that she always represents compassion and enlightenment in female form. As the female aspect of the universe, she gives birth to warmth, compassion, and relief from suffering, caring for others as a mother cares for her children. Another characteristic of her female nature is her playfulness. There are tales in which she laughs at those who take themselves too seriously or lack reverence for the feminine.

A final image from Tibetan Buddhism introduces yet another form of transformation, one quite startling to those who are unfamiliar with this tradition. In Dzogchen Buddhism, when enlightened beings proceed through the bardo after death, they may release the energy of the elements that compose the human body so that this energy is transformed back into the Five Pure Lights. This process, known as "taking the rainbow body (*jalus*)," is not considered to be symbolic. Rather, it is a state of physical mastery attainable by realized beings who are free of all delusions of substantiality and dualism. The physical manifestation of this process is that no part of the body remains except for nonliving aspects such as the hair and nails. There are several documented reports, some very recent, from witnesses to this process as the deceased travels through the bardo, a transformation that may take several days to complete.

This practice of taking the rainbow body, emerging as it does from a distant culture at the top of the world, may seem very far from the heroes' journeys of the Greeks and the resurrection story in Christianity. However, one well-known teacher of Tibetan Buddhism in the United States has suggested that Jesus himself, a being of supreme compassion and enlightenment, may have taken the rainbow body at death. Over the three days, his body would have been transformed into light, leaving only an empty tomb.[10]

We have considered transformation and rebirth from a number of perspectives, ranging from heroic transformation in the depths of hell to transformation of enlightened beings into pure light. All these perspectives share the view that the journey is never a straight-line climb. The cycles or spirals of life, death, and transformation belong, in one way or another, to all of these traditions. For the wandering hero in so-called western traditions, the cycle takes place within a lifetime (though, in the case of deities, this may be an eternal life). In the Hindu and Buddhist reincarnation traditions, each life may represent its own journey, after which the traveler returns to the bardo before undertaking another life adventure.

——————————————————{ the return }——————————————————

Once the transformation has been completed, at least for this time around, the hero still has some traveling to do. First, there is the return journey, and, finally, the hero comes home. Once the shaman has proceeded through the process of death and rebirth and acquired the essential information for healing, he or she must still make the sometimes-treacherous journey back from the spirit realm.

Perhaps for the great beings of enlightenment and compassion, it is possible to step off the wheel, enter the light, and escape the burdens of this or any world. However, for those of us walking the karmic paths, there are still many miles to go. While departing from the comforts of home may be challenging, the return threshold may be even more difficult to cross. In fact, there are some who refuse the return and choose to remain on supernatural paths. There are also those who long to return but cannot find their way.

Among these lost heroes, perhaps those who go to war are among the most poignant travelers. They answer the call to battle, typically seeking justice or protection for family and nation. They enter the unknown, seek wisdom, and face unimaginable danger in order to accomplish their objectives. They endure the unendurable and witness the indescribable. Then they turn for home, knowing that nothing will ever be the same for them.

This mythic imagery emerges from the past and catches us up in the midst of contemporary life. In our own time, we are too familiar with the stories of soldiers who cannot find a way to come home again. Where can they turn to talk about what they have seen and done? How can they explain the utter difference between what they experienced "out there" and what goes on around them in the world they used to know? How can they explain that the man or woman who departed for the battlefield is utterly different than the one who returned? It is not difficult to understand why warriors, though the battle was fierce and death was all around them, request to be returned to the field? Some talk of the thrill of danger. Others tell of needing to be back with their units rather than abandoning them. Many others relate only that they cannot find a way to live a normal life after descending so deeply into hell.

There are, of course, other ways to retreat from ordinary life. As the cultures in which we live still wage war, we struggle to understand the symptoms of Post Traumatic Stress Syndrome and confront the Thousand Yard Stare. Meanwhile, as Campbell observes regarding the mythic journey of an ancient king, the hero may choose, instead of returning, to retreat yet further from the world. "And who shall say that his decision was altogether without reason?"[11]

For those who do succeed in returning home, the journey back from the realms of the supernatural can be treacherous. Heroes are often delayed on their homeward journey, sometimes for many years. They may also find themselves pursued by those they have deceived, rejected or injured during their travels. As indicated above, they may also be reluctant, delaying their return on one pretext or another. What, then, do the stories tell us about coming home?

———————[return of odysseus]———————

Though the hero's journey is transformative, not all returns are resurrections and not all heroes descend into the underworld or rise from the dead. They are, however, returning from the realm of the unknown to territory that ought to be familiar. In many heroic accounts, however, things have changed while they have been gone. The homecoming of Odysseus is one of the most powerful narratives of the hero's return. Because his return from the Trojan wars to his home in Ithaca takes ten years, he is assumed to be dead. His son, Telemachus, goes in search for him. His wife, Penelope, has maintained hope that he will return, but numerous suitors are pursuing her, and she is running out of time.

During his journey, Odysseus consults with the dead at the underworld border, and receives advice and prophesies from Thiresias and warnings from Agamemnon that prepare him for his return. After getting hung up in various other places, a borrowed crew of Phaecian sailors finally leaves him on the home shores of Ithaca, fast asleep, where his patron goddess, Athena, finally awakens him. Upon waking, Odysseus does not recognize his homeland and worries about where to put the treasure bestowed upon him by the Phaecians. After a few mind games on both parts, Athena reveals herself to Odysseus and helps him to hide his treasure in a nearby cave. She also warns him that numerous suitors are courting his wife and seeking his throne.

Having obtained this information, Odysseus does not immediately charge back to his palace to do battle but chooses instead to resort to stealth. Athena disguises Odysseus as an old beggar and sneaks him back into his city, sending him to request shelter from an old goatherd, Eumaius, while she seeks Telemachus. Eventually, Athena finds the son of Odysseus at the house of Menelaus and persuades him to return home. Making his own return journey with the aid of Athena, Telemachus finds his way to the goatherd's home. Though he finds his father with Eumaius, Telemachus does not recognize him, even when Athena restores Odysseus to his former appearance. Eventually persuading his son that he is indeed

Odysseus, he sends Telemachus back to the palace but instructs him to tell no one of his return.

Odysseus enters the palace again disguised as an old beggar and suffers torment and humiliation from the suitors but does not reveal himself. While Odysseus is bathing, an old nurse recognizes his scar and becomes the only one to know his identity. While Odysseus has been gone, Penelope has been putting off her suitors, but she recalls a promise she had made to Odysseus to remarry if he did not return and decides she can hold out no longer. She plans a contest of strength and skill. Whoever can string Odysseus' bow and shoot through twelve axeheads will be her husband. Not surprisingly, Odysseus is the only one who is able to complete the task that Penelope has assigned, and with the help of his son and a couple of servants, he also succeeds in killing all of his rivals (and their mistresses). He then presents himself to Penelope, but she does not believe that he is Odysseus until he describes the bed that he himself had built. The two of them then weep, make love, and tell stories all night. Athena slows the night for them.

Here, again, we find a returning hero transformed beyond recognition. Even after the disguise has been lifted, neither his son nor his wife recognizes him. In fact, even when they are advised of his identity, they are skeptical, because the man before them is not the Odysseus they know. Only his old nurse knows him, recognizing his scars. That is, of course, the nature of scars. They are the permanent marks of previous suffering, and we bear them as signatures that reveal our identities, even through our various transformations.

Odysseus also returns with a treasure, but he feels a need to protect it, because he doesn't recognize his home. Without supernatural aid, it is difficult to imagine how he could have succeeded in reclaiming his authority and returning to his home and family. Though the wandering hero does eventually succeed in crossing the threshold of return, this re-entry is fraught with its own obstacles and challenges.

—————————[return to the shire]—————————

Perhaps more contemporary imagery is appropriate to conclude our discussion of the return, since this symbolism not only brings the hero back to the beginning place but also rounds out our discussion of these themes. J.R.R. Tolkien's *The Lord of the Rings* has been firing the human imagination since its first publication in 1954. More than a book (though divided into three parts, it was not conceived as a trilogy), or even a cultural phenomenon, Tolkien created a mythic realm, complete with geography and language, into which a traveler could journey along with his remarkable characters. Here, we will focus only on the return of the two characters that set out together at the beginning of the adventure, Frodo and Sam.

Both come home, along with their hobbit companions. As with Odysseus, their return is complicated by a final struggle they must face in order to recover their homeland. Their shire has been altered beyond recognition, corrupted by the malice and greed of their enemies. Before they can rest from their travels, they must bring the skills and powers they have accumulated on their journey to the task of restoring their homeland. Once this has been accomplished, they undertake the task of cleansing the territory and settling back into their former surroundings.

Frodo does his best to return to his former life. The residents of the shire care well for him, and he becomes the Deputy Mayor. However, the deep scars Frodo has acquired on his journey never quite heal, and eventually the pain becomes too much to bear. He almost finishes the record he has kept of his remarkable journey but leaves the last few pages for his faithful companion to complete. The two of them take a last journey together to the Grey Havens, where Frodo boards a white ship, along with his fellow ring-bearers, and sails away into the West. Before he departs, Sam cries out that he thought Frodo would stay home and enjoy the shire after all he had been through. Frodo's response echoes back from the most ancient tales:

> So I thought, too, once. But I have been too deeply hurt, Sam. I tried to save the Shire, and it has been saved, but not for me. It must often be so, Sam, when things are in danger: some one has to give them up, lose them, so that others may keep them.[12]

Frodo's wounds are too deep, and he cannot remain. It is Sam, his constant and faithful companion, who finally comes home. With him, we walk up the path to his home, where the lights are lit, and the evening meal is ready. He sits in his chair, takes his child from his wife and places her in his lap, and draws a deep breath:

"Well, I'm back," he says.[13]

[chapter]

LIVING IN MYTH

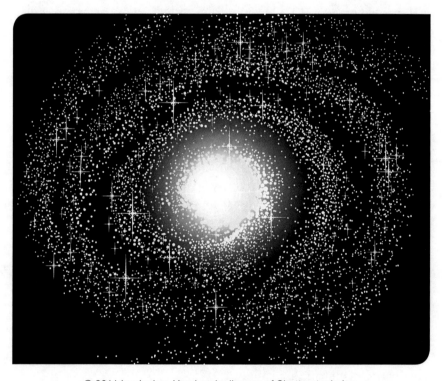

As it was in the beginning,

Is now and ever shall be,

World without end.

Gloria Patri

In prior chapters, we have explored how myths live in us. Now we turn to ways in which we live in myths. Motifs from ancient traditions can be traced through the centuries, reflected in the symbols, myths, and rituals that convey our current human responses to the deepest mysteries of our lives. Contemporary films and stories explore these mythic themes, reminding us of our strong emotional and spiritual ties to ancient narratives.

There are numerous theories regarding the cultural transitions that have taken place as human thought has developed beyond the mythic paradigm. Some scholars celebrate the triumph of the human mind in replacing primitive concepts of the supernatural with a more rational and scientific worldview. Others mourn the loss of deeper meaning as human cultures learn to respond to mystery with logic and magic with scorn.

Have we really left the mythic realm so far behind, or have we just forgotten how to recognize it? Even when we are not consciously seeking contact with myths, are there ways in which our contemporary lives still reflect the mythic imagination?

———————————[totems]———————————

Aside from certain new age movements and neo-pagan traditions, contemporary culture no longer views the human relationship with animals in terms of kinship or sacred bonds. Although our indigenous populations may see things differently, we typically do not believe our ancestors to be of another species, and we do not seek guidance from spirit animals. However, many individuals maintain extraordinary relationships with animals, and quite a few of us have totems, whether we realize it or not.

Some people fill their houses with photos, images, and symbols of an animal or plant that has a special meaning for them. When asked why images of elephants or roses or frogs or horses or dogs fill their homes, the reply is often vague or uncertain. "I don't know. I just like them." When visiting a zoo or wild animal park, we may feel ourselves drawn to certain creatures, unable to tear ourselves away. Animals may cross our path or behave in unusual ways around us, and we may find certain animals particularly frightening or fascinating.

Many studies now support the claim that contact with certain animals can be very beneficial for reducing human stress, depression, and anxiety, and hospitals and nursing homes have implemented programs utilizing therapy animals to benefit their patients. There are even studies indicating that some animals, such as dogs, experience biological benefits from being in the company of humans.

Animals still interact with us in ways that defy scientific analysis. Stroking their fur reduces our blood pressure. We feel an emotional stirring when they gaze into our eyes. They come to us in our dreams. Sometimes we choose them as companions, but we also have a vague sense that they are choosing us.

———————————————[the wild]———————————————

When the United States Congress passed the Wilderness Act in 1964 (Pub-L 88-577), they affirmed the definition of wilderness as "an area where the earth and its community of life are untrammeled by man, where man himself is a visitor who does not remain." Wilderness was thereby distinguished from those areas where humans and their works dominate the landscape. By this act, some nine million acres of public land were designated as wilderness and protected, as much as possible, from human manipulation. The concept was that these environments might operate according to the forces of nature, unrestrained and unaltered by human interference.

When our European ancestors and their descendants pressed westward across the North American continent, they had no desire to preserve the wild. The wilderness was considered to be a dark and sinister place, without physical or spiritual comfort. Bereft of law, religion, or civilization, early pioneers felt that corruption and seduction were ever-present dangers, and morality required that this land be conquered and civilized so that Christianity and progress could prevail. To civilize the wilderness meant bringing light to darkness, order to chaos, and moral values to the lawless wastes. This commitment to domesticating the savage land and transforming it for human use is certainly alive and well in contemporary life, so why would the United States develop an interest in preserving land where humans only visit and do not remain?

As noted earlier, there were once thousands of indigenous cultures across the North American continent, and many of them had a more integrated and intimate relationship with the land. Just as it is an error to assume the existence of a generic Native American, it is problematic to gloss over the wide variety of ways in which these cultures interacted with their environments. However, just as many native cultures preserved a more intimate and spiritual kinship with animals, there is strong evidence that early indigenous cultures considered the land to be a gift that could not or should not be bought and sold.

Thoreau famously stated, "In wildness is the preservation of the World." Wilderness is by definition outside of the structures of the ordered

and chaotic place occupied by "the other."[1] When we come
with natural forces outside of human control, we share this ex-
with every human culture that has preceded us. Obviously, these
were here before human life arrived. Perhaps less obviously, they
very likely still be here after human life has either evolved into some-
ng else or self-destructed into extinction.

As noted in the first chapter, myths often demonstrate a startling similarity to one another, even in very diverse times and places. The natural
imagery that moved our ancestors to explore its spiritual power still stirs
in us a vague but powerful yearning. We search the sky at dusk, looking
for the first star to make our wish. We stand gazing at waves, sunrises and
sunsets, plants bending toward the light, and we respond not just with ad-
miration for their beauty but with an unidentified emotion that is love but
also something more.

—————————————[the great round]—————————————

Aside from religious rituals, perhaps our closest present day association
with the mythic, just as in the ancient past, comes to us through the cycle
of the seasons. Though we are often unaware of it, the traditions through
which we mark certain times of the year are laden with images directly
connecting us to our ancient human past. These annual rituals cannot, of
course, be completely separated from religious practice, since so many of
our seasonal rites are intimately linked with religious beliefs. For purposes
of this discussion, however, we will primarily focus on traditions and rituals that link us back to the mythic past.

Separation of the sacred from other aspects of life is not, of course,
any part of the mythic worldview. As far back as we can trace the mythic
imagination, there have always been sacred times and sacred places. As
we have seen, primal people were connected to their totemic relatives
and maintained a religious rapport with the spiritual powers of the natural
world, while ritual enabled them, as Berry so aptly stated, "to enter into the
grand liturgy of the universe."[2] As spiritual traditions developed or settled
into a new area, they practiced their rituals at sites where earlier cultures
had built their sacred shrines and temples. Layer after layer of religious
ritual and belief builds upon ancient beliefs and practices. Cultures do
build their religious sites on top of former places of worship for political
and even military reasons, to emphasize their dominance. However, it is
also true that human beings find themselves drawn to mark certain seasons
and to make contact with the divine at certain locations, because there is
something about them that moves us and inspires us. This is no less so now

than it has been through the ages. Circling around the seasons, we find that contemporary rituals have ancient roots. Here we will consider our mythic responses to the seasons of winter and the dying and rising of the light.

———————————[the dying time]———————————

We begin our exploration of annual mythic practice in contemporary life not at what might seem the beginning (springtime) but where some ancient cultures placed it—at harvest time.[3] As we have seen throughout our exploration of myth, any new life in the mythic world must be preceded by death.

Just as underworld deities are also gods of the harvest, autumn is both the time of gathering in and of dying off. At summer's end, the long days grow shorter, and the fullness of the earth turns almost imperceptibly toward the dying time. Many ancient cultures acknowledged this season with appropriate rituals.

For the Celts, the new year began with the festival of Samhain (pronounced sow'in), originally Samuin, at dusk on the night of the full October moon (the blood moon). Eventually, the tradition became associated with the Christian festival known as All Saint's Day, All Soul's Day, or All Hallow's Eve and was fixed on October 31-November 1. Rituals at this time celebrated both summer's end and the beginning of winter.

Just as the year began when the dark of winter approached, the day began at the beginning of night. At this time, the veil between the world of the living and the dead was at its thinnest, and the souls of the dead could pass between worlds. Among other motifs, autumn festivals were associated with placating the supernatural powers of nature. There is some evidence that Celtic villagers gathered the best of the harvest and prepared a feast for the dead at this time. Another typical aspect of the celebration was the building of a great fire. Animals that could not be kept through the winter were slaughtered, and their bones were cast into the flames.[4]

This season was also associated with oracles and divination. For Celts, the hazelnut was a particular symbol of wisdom, associated with ancient goddesses, and could be used to foretell the future. Another tradition probably associated with spirits was the wearing of masks and costumes, although speculation abounds regarding their meaning. They may have been used as disguises to fool the spirits or to frighten them. There is some evidence that villagers representing the dead paraded to the edge of town in costume to draw the spirits away from their homes.[5]

Contemporary customs associated with the harvest season have pagan roots. Apples, nuts, and other fruits, typical centerpieces of the season, can be associated with the Roman harvest feast of Pomona, goddess of fruit. Bobbing for apples has been associated with everything from divining one's future marriage partner to attaining immortality. Other seasonal imagery such as pumpkins, cornhusks, and scarecrows are also obviously associated with the harvest.

Aside from Halloween, there are other festivals in many cultures that acknowledge the dying time. One well-known festival is the Mexican celebration known as the Day of the Dead (*Dia de los Muertos*). Families gather to pray for the souls of the dead and build private altars with offerings of sugar skulls, marigolds, and the deceased's favorite foods and beverages. These offerings are also made at the gravesites. This festival may well have originated with Aztec rites and indigenous rituals dating back thousands of years. In addition to Mexican and Latin American cultures, similar observances can be found in Europe, Asia, and Africa.

—————————————[the long dark]—————————————

Ovid recorded a myth associated with the winter solstice and the ancient belief that cultures in the Northern Hemisphere experience two weeks of calm weather in the middle of December. According to this tale, Aeolus, ruler of the winds, had a daughter named Alcyone. Her husband, Ceyx, the king of Thessaly, was drowned at sea, and Alcyone was overcome by grief and threw herself into the sea. Instead of drowning, however, the winds carried her to her husband. The gods transformed them both into winter birds, and when Alcyone lays her eggs and sits upon her floating nest, her father calms every storm and hushes every wind so that she and her children will be safe.

The only vestige of this myth in contemporary culture is the expression "halcyon days," not much in use, to mean calm and peaceful days. Most often, it is associated with nostalgia for an idyllic time in the past.

It is significant that this time of stillness is mythically located in the deep of winter. This is the time of the long dark, when night and cold bring a great stillness to the world. Animals sleep in the depths of their caves and burrows. Plant life, though appearing to have succumbed to death, actually lies dormant, waiting for the return of the light. In the depths of the soil, seeds quietly open. Even though death seems to have captured the earth, the world is actually turning toward a new beginning.

Mythic acknowledgment of this deepening time took place all over the world, and many vestiges of these ancient traditions are still with us. Not surprisingly, ancient cultures typically associated winter solstice celebrations with the sun and the sun's return. By 274 CE, the Roman emperor

Aurelian had reformed and elevated a cult devoted to Sol Invictus, the late Roman Empire's sun god, alongside other traditional Roman cults such as those devoted to Apollo and Mithras. Some scholars claim that Emperor Constantine declared December 25 as the date of Christ's birth as part of a strategy to win over the pagan Romans to Christianity, because they were already celebrating the birth of the sun on that day. Constantine was devoted to the symbol of the unconquerable sun and carried the image on his coins and banners, but there is no clear evidence that the festival of Sol Invictus was celebrated on that date.

For the Germanic and Scandinavian people, the Yule fest, celebrated from late December to early January, marked the end of the long nights and the beginning of the light's return. As an indigenous celebration, it probably included feasting, singing and sacrifices for a fertile and peaceful return of the light. The English historian Bede also notes an Anglo-Saxon pagan celebration on December 25, marking the beginning of the year with an all-night celebration called "mothers'" night and honoring the divine mothers.

Saturnalia, an ancient Roman celebration, also took place at this time. Held in honor of Cronus (Saturn), father of the major Greek and Roman gods, the celebration lasted a week and also included sacrifices and feasting, as well as holiday dress and the exchange of small gifts. Although it is not clear whether living trees were brought into the home, this celebration was marked by decorating homes with evergreen boughs and decorating living trees with precious metals. Evergreen trees and boughs are, of course, symbols of everlasting life. For Egypt, a land without evergreens in the traditional sense, the palm tree symbolized resurrection and was associated with the phoenix. Egyptians therefore followed a similar custom of decorating their homes with palm branches during the winter solstice, honoring the death and resurrection of Osiris.

Eventually, the Yuletide celebration became equivalent to the Christian Christmas celebration, and a number of contemporary traditions can be directly traced to ancient pagan celebrations. Feasting, caroling, and the burning of a Yule log are still practiced. Especially in Scandinavia, ancient pagan symbols such as the Yule Goat and the Yule Boar are still in use at Christmastime.

Early Christians did not typically celebrate Jesus' birth and some leaders opposed any form of celebration to mark the event. Origin held that birthdays were for pagan gods, and Christians should not honor Christ with traditions similar to those honoring secular kings and rulers.

Even among those who advocated this celebration, the date was much debated. The eventual choice of December 25 by the Western church possibly indicated an association between the celestial sun and the son of God. Whether or not celebrations devoted to Sol Invictus and Mithras, the Iranian "Sun of Righteousness," were being celebrated on that date, most scholars agree that Western Christians began to celebrate Christmas on December 25 around 336 CE, after Constantine declared Christianity to be the favored religion of the empire.

Interestingly, the early Christian church opposed the decoration of houses with evergreen boughs and the cutting and decorating of trees, because such practices were part of pagan traditions. The prophet Jeremiah very specifically condemned certain "false customs:"

> [A] tree from the forest is cut down, and worked with an ax by the hands of an artisan; people deck it with silver and gold; they fasten it with hammer and nails so that it cannot move. Their idols are like scarecrows in a cucumber field, and they cannot speak; they have to be carried, for they cannot walk. Do not be afraid of them, for they cannot do evil, nor is it in them to do good. (Jeremiah 10:3-5)

Church leaders, from Tertullian to the English Puritans, condemned a number of customs associated with Christmas as heathen traditions or pagan mockery, including the use of lamps, wreaths, holly, mistletoe, Christmas carols, decorated trees, and even joyful expression.

In 1851, a German Lutheran pastor in Cleveland, Ohio, was the first to decorate a Christmas tree in an American church. Though some members of his German congregation were pleased, others were shocked, calling the practice heathenish and idolatrous. Within five years, Christmas trees could be found all over the country.

Clearly, Christmas traditions with ancient non-Christian roots are a common part of the holiday throughout the world. Certain Christian groups still reject the holiday and its traditions because of these connections to pagan celebrations. Many other Christians have re-interpreted these symbols and integrated them into their beliefs. The heart-shaped leaves of ivy reflect God's incarnation on earth, while the thorns and red berries of the holly represent Christ's crown of thorns and the blood he shed. Garlands, wreaths, and evergreens all bring to mind Christ's promise of eternal life, and lighted candles stand for the light of God coming into the world.

The adoption and adaptation of ancient motifs and traditions need not be viewed as contamination or heresy. Clearly, the truths implicit in these symbols are not diminished by their context. Humans interacting with the natural world have the capacity to see beyond the object or phenomenon to the deeper meanings within. It has always been this way. These traditions develop out of our response to all that moves us, and their meanings carry forward through the ages.

————————————[return of the light]————————————

If the mid-winter is the quietest time of the year, the spring equinox is definitely a mythic wakeup call. Though perhaps a bit sluggish at first, the world eventually wakes in a riot of light, color, and new life. We symbol-making creatures have never been hesitant to celebrate.

Many ancient pagan traditions around the Mediterranean probably celebrated with enthusiastic festivals at the vernal equinox. Attis, Adonis, Dionysus, and Tammuz, along with the yearly rebirth of vegetation associated with them, were probably honored at this time. As noted earlier, Attis was said to be born of a virgin and to have died and been resurrected. Some scholars place the celebration of this event between March 22 and March 25 of the Julian calendar. Worship of Cybele came to Rome late in the third century BCE, and Christian worship of Jesus and pagan worship of Attis probably took place at the same time in the same geographical area.

Archaeologists believe that vernal equinox celebrations may be as much as 12,000 years old, although some consider these events to be still more ancient. There is evidence that the ancestors of Celtic and Anglo-Saxon cultures celebrated both the spring and fall equinox, and Persians, along with other cultures, celebrated the new year at this time. Astarte, the Chaldean queen of heaven, counterpart of Ishtar, was also likely celebrated with springtime festivities.

Scholars take various positions regarding the origin of the term Easter to refer to the Christian holiday. Many claim that the name is of pagan origin and very likely referred to a goddess of spring and the sacrifices and celebrations devoted to her. The deity most often named is Eostre (also Ostara, Eastur, and Eastra, among others), an Anglo-Saxon goddess. The Venerable Bede (672-735 CE), a Christian scholar of the early eighth century, asserted that Easter was named after the goddess Eostre, a mother goddess of dawn and fertility. He also noted that rituals devoted to her had died out and been replaced by Paschal celebrations and that one of the Anglo-Saxon months, Eosturmonath, had been named for her.

Whether such a goddess actually existed is a matter of debate. Various sources also attribute the origin of a number of additional terms to her, including estrus, estrogen, East and the month of April, although there is little or no evidence to support these claims. Other goddess names are also in the running as the origin of the term Easter, including Astarte or Ashtaroth, the Phoenician goddess of fertility and sexual love, who became identified with Ishtar, Isis, and Aphrodite, among others.

The association between the Jewish celebration of Passover and Easter is much stronger. In most European languages, the name for the Christian holiday celebrating Jesus's resurrection is similar or identical to the term for Passover. The term *pascha,* for example (a term used for Easter in several countries), came from the Chaldean or Aramaean form of the Hebrew Passover festival, *pesach.* Jesus celebrated Passover with his disciples, and early Christians, most of whom were Jewish, continued the ritual. Eventually, this sacred meal became associated with the Christian communion ritual. Sacrifices of lambs in the temple became associated with the sacrifice of the Paschal Lamb.

Some contemporary Easter and springtime symbols are so clearly linked to ancient traditions of fertility and rebirth that the association really needs no external support. Anyone who breeds rabbits will tell you that there is a very good reason why these creatures are fertility symbols. And given our discussion of the association between creation stories and cosmic eggs, perhaps the ubiquity of egg symbols at this time of year also needs no additional explanation. Flowers, too, seem obvious links between ancient equinox celebrations and contemporary springtime displays.

Certain ancient cultural practices do, however, provide us with additional insight into these symbols. In the ancient world, it is the hare rather than the rabbit that has a central place. (The term "bunny" can probably be applied to either animal.) It appears in ancient cultures all over the world, almost always representing the moon, the rising sun, fertility, and immortality as well as cunning and bravery. Osiris was related to the hare and was sacrificed in the form of a hare to guarantee the annual flooding of the Nile, essential to Egyptian agriculture. The Native American Michabo (the Great Hare) was creator of the world, god of the dawn, and preserver of life. The hare was also associated with several goddesses, including the Norse Frejya and the Celtic Cerridwin and is sometimes depicted in the company of Venus and Amor.

As for the egg, it was a symbol of new life in many cultures, ranging from ancient Egypt to Polynesia. In addition to the cosmic egg, there are numerous accounts of deities, as well as heroes and demons, emerging from eggs. Cultures ranging from the Druids to the Chinese decorated and exchanged eggs. Ostrich eggs, sometimes decorated with paint or incised lines, have been found in Egyptian tombs, and clay eggs have been found in prehistoric tombs in Sweden and Russia. Because of the obvious imagery of new life breaking out of a cold, hard enclosure, the egg has often been associated with rebirth from the tomb. The ancient word for the inner coffin in Egyptian burial places means "egg," and Christians associate the egg with Christ coming forth from the tomb.

Because of their characteristics, flowers have obviously been associated with beauty, fragility, and sweet scent. Because they appear with the return of the sun, they are associated with birth. Because they fade and wilt quickly, they are associated with death. The anemone is associated with the death and rebirth of Adonis, and carnations are the flowers of the dead in Mexico. The lily was a symbol of Isis, Hera, and Venus. In the Homeric hymn to Demeter, the poet sings the praises of the narcissus, a marvelous and radiant flower planted by Zeus on behalf of Hades to snare the lovely Persephone as she playfully picked flowers in a meadow along with other "big breasted daughters of Oceanos:"[6]

> It astonished everyone who saw it, immortal gods and mortal men alike. From its root it pushed up a hundred heads and a fragrance from its top making all the vast sky above smile, and all the earth, and all the salt swelling of the sea. And she was astonished too, she stretched out both her hands to pick this delightful thing. [7]

This text also emphasizes the strong association between certain flowers and sexuality or seduction. Though the lily is now considered a symbol of purity, the Greeks associated the lily with sexuality, and the orchid (with a name derived from the Greek word for testicle) was believed to control sexuality and the gender of unborn children.

The return of the light has also been celebrated from ancient times to the present with fire, in the form of candles and bonfires. Many other springtime traditions have been associated with ancient rituals of new birth, including wearing new garments and baking honey cakes or buns marked with a symbol to honor the reborn deity.

———————————[cosmos]————————————

In 1986, a year prior to his death, Joseph Campbell published a book entitled *The Inner Reaches of Outer Space: Metaphor as Myth and as Religion.* In this text, he reflects upon the relationship between ancient cosmogonies and contemporary theories regarding the origin of the universe. Recalling his thoughts while watching the Apollo mission to the moon and seeing Armstrong's boot touch down on the surface, it occurred to him "that outer space is within inasmuch as the laws of space are within us: outer and inner space are the same." Human beings are actually born from space, since our galaxy, including our sun, took form out of primordial space, and the earth is a "flying satellite of that sun." Humans are productions of the earth. "We are, as it were, its organs. Our eyes are the eyes of this earth; our knowledge is the earth's knowledge. And the earth, as we now know, is a production of space."[8]

Being a man of myth, Campbell observed a resemblance between scientific accounts of the Big Bang and Ovid's cosmogony in *Metamorphoses*. In Ovid's narrative, the original state was a vaguely floating, formless chaos until a divine force (*deus*) brought order out of chaos and sent all the elements to their proper places. Physicists and astronomers describe the state before creation as a great featureless mass or "impulse" (Campbell compares this to *deus*). When this mass reached its maximum concentration, "the inconceivable pressure of an entire incipient universe confined to a single point became converted into energy and mass, the primal twin manifestations of all perceived 'reality' in what is known to the mind as space-time...."[9]

The relationship between these narrations of the beginning brought Campbell to an important realization regarding what he calls "the wonderland of myth:" "From the outer world the senses carry images to the mind, which do not become myth, however, until there transformed by fusion with accordant insights, awakened as imagination from the inner world of the body."[10]

And so we come round again to the place this text began, with our metaphorical minds. As we have learned from the myths, however, no return is final. Much has happened since Campbell watched the moon landing, and more contemporary discoveries have taken our cosmic explorations to a whole new level.

Author Duane Elgin makes specific use of the hero's journey paradigm to describe this co-evolution of culture and consciousness from earlier mechanistic views to a new awareness. Humanity has already been through a long and tumultuous cultural journey, and its various stages eventually took us far from the mythic sense of natural connection to the powers of life. The "existential mindset of the industrial era bleached the life out of nature and left a machine-like cosmos filled mostly with dead matter and empty space."[11]

Newtonian physics and European philosophy combined to establish this mechanistic paradigm, providing alternative factual accounts to explain natural events. Brian Swimme, for example, notes that science provides us with information about the sun's transformation of energy, but nothing in science enables us to take it in. "It is yet another forbidding truth about the inhuman universe, and we unconsciously commit ourselves to the modern disaster of sealing ourselves away from the universe."[12]

The cultural historian Thomas Berry summarizes the cultural losses that have accompanied intellectual gains:

> Our scientific preoccupations and relentless commercial
> exploitation of the planet have left us with diminished sensitivity
> to the natural world in the deeper emotional, aesthetic, mythic and
> mystical communication it is offering to us. We are so enclosed in
> our human world that we have almost completely lost our intimacy
> with the natural world.[13]

Perhaps Einstein and his contemporaries first rocked this mechanistic boat, but more recent discoveries may take us into territory only mythic imagery can describe. The observational sciences have shattered the mechanistic paradigm, proposing theories to account for a universe that doesn't always operate in predictable ways: relativity, quantum physics, Heisenberg's uncertainty principle, chaos theories, and now even string theories. Scientists have reached more deeply than ever into realms ranging from the inconceivably tiny to the unimaginably vast, and the data they have found defy any objective description. To add to the mystery, there is a new wrinkle to all these observations. It seems that on some level we alter "reality" by observing it.

Berry notes that these recent scientific endeavors introduce a "new sense of the sacred dimension of the universe and of the planet Earth." Where once we sought the objective truth of the universe, we now realize "that there is subjectivity in all our knowledge and that we ourselves, precisely as intelligent beings, activate one of the deepest dimensions of the universe." Knowledge is less about the relationship of subjects and objects than it is "a communion of subjects."

"As we open to this new understanding of the universe, aliveness and awe return to the world around us." This new awareness sparks an "intuition that a living presence permeates the universe" and sustains all forms of life, including human life.[14]

As we explore these new discoveries, we come to realize what our most ancient predecessors may have understood: That "the universe process, the Earth process, and the human process constitute a single unbroken sequence of transformations."[15] That the living universe is more like a web than a ladder, everything is connected, and the spiritual and physical worlds are not vastly separated but intimately related. What does it mean that the oldest stories we discover and the newest stories we relate about the nature of things are eerily similar? Is this the return of the human species to our home in the universe?

The answer to that question has yet to play out. Even if we are re-discovering the power of the mythic image to evoke our ancient and evolving relationship to the universe, the cycles always bring us to a new beginning. Cosmic travelers now, we are about to cross the threshold and commence a new journey. Perhaps the spirits of the ancient ones wait at the crossroads to share bits of cryptic wisdom. Perhaps gods and demons, angels and monsters are even now making plans to bless us or curse us or eat us alive. We hear the call and set out again, and all the forces of chaos and creation stir restlessly and wonder.

ENDNOTES

————————————[chapter 1]————————————

[1] Ralph Waldo Emerson, "The Poet," in *Essays* (Boston: Houghton, Mifflin & Co., 1865), 20.

[2] Ernst Cassirer, *Language and Myth* (New York: Dover Publications, Inc., 1946), 8. Translated by Susanne K. Langer.

[3] Cassirer, 38.

[4] Susanne Langer, *Philosophy in a New Key* (London: Oxford University Press, 1942, 1951),28.

[5] Langer, 41.

[6] Nelle Morton, "The Goddess as Metaphoric Image" in *The Journey is Home* (Boston: Beacon Press, 1985), 152

[7] Charles Long, *Alpha: the Myths of Creation* (copyright 1963 by Charles Long, reprinted by Scholars Press, 1983), 10.

[8] Victor Turner, "Symbolic Studies," *Annual Review of Anthropology,* vol. 4 (1975), 155.

[9] The first psychologists to study perception in this way were Johann Wolfgang von Goethe, Ernst Mach, Christian von Ehrenfels, Max Wertheimer, Wolfgang Kohler, Kurt Koffka, and Kurt Lewin. As national socialism interrupted their work in the German-speaking world, several of these theorists immigrated to the United States to continue their work. E. Rubin originally published theory on figure-ground perception in German in 1915.

[10] Other researchers working on this issue include Daniel Weissman, Glenn Wilson, Gloria Mark and Alan Keen.

[11] George Lakoff and Mark Johnson, *Metaphors We Live By* (Chicago: The University of Chicago Press, 1980, 2003), 193.

[12] Karen Armstrong, *A Short History of Myth* (Edinburgh: Canongate, 2006), 4.

[13] Joseph Campbell, *The Inner Reaches of Outer Space: Metaphor As Myth and As Religion* (Novato: New World Library, 1986, 2002), xx.

[14] Campbell, 28-29.

[15] Paul Ricoeur, *Symbolism of Evil* (Boston: Beacon Press, 1967), 5.

[16] William G. Doty, *Myth: a Handbook* (Westport, CT: Greenwood Press, 2004), 9.

[17] Thomas Berry, *The Sacred Universe* (New York: Columbia University Press, 2009), 54-55.

[18] See Morton, 30.

[19] Armstrong, pp. 31-33.

[20] Campbell, 7.

[21] Campbell, xiv.

[22] Contrary to popular belief, for example, Inuit people do not have more words for snow than English-speaking people.

[23] Catherine Bell, *Ritual Theory, Ritual Practice* (New York: Oxford University Press), 92.

[24] Emile Durkheim, *The Elementary Forms of Religious Life* (New York: Collier Books, 1961), 464.

[25] Armstrong, 23.

[26] Armstrong, 36.

[27] Ibid.
[28] Berry, 105.
[29] Clifford Geertz, *The Interpretation of Cultures* (New York: Basic Books, 1973), 112.
[30] Terry Eagleton, *Literary Theory, an Introduction* (Minneapolis: University of Minnesota Press 1983), 116.
[31] Durkheim, 414.
[32] Durkheim, 427.
[33] Bell, 92.
[34] Leonard Cohen, from "Stories of the Street."

──────────────[chapter 2]──────────────

[1] Long, 18.
[2] Long, 23.
[3] Probably the best-known system is Charles H. Long's division into five categories: emergence, world-parent, creation from chaos and the cosmic egg, creation from nothing, and earth-diver myths. More recent typologies have been created by Marta Weigle and Raymond Van Over.
[4] There is a lively discussion about the actual meaning of this word and its companion word for creation in Genesis. Some scholars have suggested that *bara* may refer to an action more like extending or even separating. Most agree that the word refers to the act of creation in general.
[5] Long, 30.
[6] Long, 37.
[7] Long, 38.
[8] Long, 40.
[9] Long, 68.
[10] Mircea Eliade, *Myths, Dream and Mysteries* (London: Harvill Press, 1960), 183.
[11] Eliade, 184.
[12] Philip Freund, *Myths of Creation* (New York: Washington Square Press, Inc., 1965), 97-8.
[13] Joseph Campbell, *The Masks of God: Primitive Mythology* (New York: Viking Press, 1959), 181.
[14] Campbell, 181-2.
[15] Mircea Eliade, *The Myth of the Eternal Return,* Bollingen Series XLVI (New York: Pantheon Books, 1954), 20.
[16] Long, 224.
[17] Completed in 713 CE, the *Kojiki* was created under the auspices of the imperial court. Its title directly translates as "Record of Ancient Things."
[18] Stephanie Dalley, trans., *Myths from Mesopotamia: Creation, the Flood, Gilgamesh, and Others* (Oxford: Oxford University Press, 1989, rev. 2000), 243.
[19] Dalley, 254-5.
[20] Bernhard W. Anderson, *Creation versus Chaos, the Reinterpretation of Mythical Symbolism in the Bible* (New York: Association Press, 1967), 29.
[21] Donald L. Philippi, trans., *Kojiki* (Tokyo: University of Tokyo Press, 1968), 49.
[22] The name may literally mean "self-curdling island" and apparently was thought to be near what is now Osaka Bay.
[23] *Kojiki,* 50.
[24] Philippi's translation has "how good a lad" and "how good a maiden."

———————————{ chapter 3 }———————————

[1] Joseph Campbell, *The Hero with a Thousand Faces* (Princeton: Princeton University Press, 1949, 1968), 30.

[2] See Joseph Campbell, *Pathways to Bliss: Mythology and Personal Transformation,* edited by David Kudler (Novato, California: New World Library, 2004), 145, 159.

[3] See, for example, Maureen Murdock, *The Heroine's Journey* (Boston: Shambhala, 1990) and Carol S. Pearson, *The Hero Within* (New York: Harper Collins, 1986).

[4] Campbell, *Hero with a Thousand Faces,* 29.

[5] Campbell, 39.

[6] Campbell, 37.

[7] Campbell, 58.

[8] Ibid.

[9] Campbell, 82.

[10] Campbell, 185. Campbell notes that this passage was missing from the standard Assyrian edition of the legend but appears in a much earlier Babylonian fragmentary text.

[11] Mircea Eliade, *Myths, Dreams, and Mysteries* (New York: Harper & Row, 1960), 200.

[12] Eliade, *Myths, Dreams, and Mysteries,* 208.

[13] I thank my friend and mentor, Dan Rhoades of Claremont School of Theology, for this simple but profound observation.

[14] Campbell, 216.

[15] Mircea Eliade, *Birth and Rebirth* (New York: Harper & Bros., 1958), xiii.

[16] Eliade, *Birth and Rebirth,* 64-65.

[17] Joan Halifax, *Shaman: the Wounded Healer* (London: Thames & Hudson Ltd., 1982), 18.

[18] Joan Halifax, *Shamanic Voices: A Survey of Visionary Narratives* (New York: E.P. Dutton, 1979), 5.

[19] Halifax, 14.

[20] Mircea Eliade, *Shamanism* (New York: Pantheon Books, 1964), 36.

[21] Halifax, *Shaman: The Wounded Healer,* 18.

[22] Campbell, 193.

[23] Christine Downing, *Psyche's Sisters* (San Francisco: Harper & Row, 1988), 47-48.

[24] Psyche had never before been personified in Greek and Roman mythology, although Venus and Cupid were, of course, well known deities. Apuleius would have been familiar with the meaning of the term in archaic Greek: the essential aspect of the soul that was not dependent on the human body. His characterization of Psyche as a mortal female has caused many scholars to analyze this story in terms of female awakening.

[25] See, for example, Maria Gimbutas, *The Language of the Goddess* (San Francisco: Harper & Row, 1989).

[26] Christine Downing, *Goddess: Mythological Images of the Feminine* (New York: Continuum, 1996), 9.

[27] Ibid.

[28] Downing, 12.

[29] It should be noted that the term "crone" is used here to refer to a female figure with ancient wisdom and skill in the healing arts rather than any more derogatory understanding of the term.

[30] Scott Leonard and Michael McClure, *Myth & Knowing* (New York: McGraw-Hill, 2004). This text has a very thorough discussion of this approach.

[31] Downing, 12.
[32] Gimbutas, xix.
[33] Carol Christ, *Odyssey with the Goddess* (New York: Continuum, 1995), 2.
[34] Leonard and McClure, 189.
[35] Eliade, *Patterns in Comparative Religion,* 38.
[36] Eliade, *Patterns in Comparative Religion,* 39.
[37] Ibid.
[38] Leonard and McClure, 189.
[39] All Biblical quotes are from the New Revised Standard Version.
[40] St. Anselm, *The Oxford Guide to the Book of Common Prayer,* Charles C. Hefling, Cynthia L. Shattuck, eds. (Oxford: Oxford University Press, 2006), 457.
[41] David Leeming and Jake Page, *God: Myths of the Male Divine* (New York: Oxford University Press, 1996), 34-35.
[42] Eliade, *Myths, Dreams, and Mysteries,* 199.

──────────────────────[chapter 4]──────────────────────

[1] Karen Armstrong, *A Short History of Myth* (Edinburgh: Canongate, 2006), 3-4.
[2] Armstrong, 59.
[3] G. Van der Leeuw, "Primordial Time and Final Time," Papers from the *Eranos Yearbooks,* vol. 3, 338.
[4] Ibid.
[5] Joseph Campbell, *Hero with a Thousand Faces,* 105.
[6] Diane Wolkstein and Samuel Noah Kramer, *Inanna, Queen of Heaven and Earth* (New York: Harper & Row, 1983).
[7] Wolkstein and Kramer, 156.
[8] It should be noted that male dress might also indicate power or status. Joseph's coat of many colors indicated his higher status in his family.
[9] Wolkstein and Kramer, 54.
[10] Wolkstein and Kramer, 55.
[11] Wolkstein and Kramer, 56.
[12] Wolkstein and Kramer, 57.
[13] Wolkstein and Kramer, 60.
[14] Wolkstein and Kramer, 62.
[15] Ibid.
[16] Wolkstein and Kramer, 63.
[17] Wolkstein and Kramer, 67.
[18] Wolkstein and Kramer, 68.
[19] Wolkstein and Kramer, 71.
[20] Joseph Campbell, *The Hero with a Thousand Faces,* 108.
[21] Ibid, 108.
[22] John H Leith (ed.), *Creeds of the Churches* (Atlanta: John Knox Press, 1963), 24.
[23] "Introductory Commentary by His Holiness the XIVth Dalai Lama," *The Tibetan Book of the Dead* (New York: Penguin Books, (2006), xxviii.
[24] I would like to thank Tara McKibben for this insight. Working with patients diagnosed with Alzheimer's, she often experienced them as living in a transitional state, no longer quite in this world.

[25] Narada Mahathera, quoted in *The Wheel of Death,* Philip Kapleau, ed. (New York: Harper Torchbooks, 1971), 17.

[26] Timothy K. Beal, *Religion and Its Monsters* (New York: Routledge, 2002), 26.

[27] Beal, p. 195.

[28] Ibid.

[29] Ibid.

[30] Beal, 50.

————————————[chapter 5]————————————

[1] Joseph Campbell, *Hero with a Thousand Faces,* 226.

[2] Campbell, 216.

[3] Ibid.

[4] Ibid.

[5] J Gwyn Griffiths, "Osiris," *The Ancient Gods Speak,* Donald B. Redford, ed. (Oxford and New York: Oxford University Press, 2002), 305.

[6] *The Egyptian Book of the Dead: The Book of Going Forth By Day,* ed. Eva von Dassow, trans. Raymond O. Faulkner ((San Francisco: Chronicle Books, 2008), 106.

[7] Eliade, *Myth of the Eternal Return,* 130.

[8] Robert A. Armour, *Gods and Myths of Ancient Egypt* (Cairo, New York: the American University in Cairo Press, 1986), 1.

[9] *The Bhagavad Gita,* trans. Eknath Easwaran (Tomales: CA: Nilgiri Press, 1985, 2007), 117.

[10] Conversation with Tsultrim Allione, spiritual director of Tara Mandala, a Buddhist retreat center near Pagosa Springs in Southern Colorado.

[11] Campbell, *Hero with a Thousand Faces,* 196.

[12] J.R.R. Tolkien, *The Lord of the Rings* (Boston: Houghton Mifflin Co, 1998. Copyright by J.R.R. Tolkien, 1955), 1006.

[13] Tolkien, 1008.

————————————[chapter 6]————————————

[1] Frederick C. Tiffany, "Facing the Wilderness/Encountering Chaos," *Quarterly Review* (Spring, 1998). 55.

[2] Thomas Berry, *The Sacred Universe* (New York: Columbia University Press, 2009), 104.

[3] Though perhaps the association is more commercial than mythical, in the United States, Halloween is typically considered to be the beginning of the holiday season.

[4] The term "bonfire" is probably derived from bane-fire or bone-fire.

[5] The common belief that Samhain is the name for an ancient Celtic god of the dead is erroneous, although some conservative Christian groups base their opposition to Halloween on this false belief.

[6] "To Demeter (I)," *The Homeric Hymns,* trans. Charles Boer (Kingston, Rhode Island and London: Asphodel Press, 1970, 2004, 2006), 110.

[7] "To Demeter (I)," 111.

[8] Joseph Campbell, *The Inner Reaches of Outer Space: Metaphor As Myth and As Religion* (Novato, CA: New World Library, 1986, 2002), 2.

[9] Campbell, 3.

[10] Campbell, 5.

[11] Duane Elgin, *The Living Universe* (San Francisco: Berrett-Koehler Publishers, Inc., 2009), 142.

[12] Swimme, 40.

[13] Berry, 104.

[14] Berry, 106.

[15] Ibid.

WEBSITES WITH COMPLETE TEXTS

————————————[Amor & Psyche]————————————

http://www.euphoniousmonks.com/amor.htm
http://www.pitt.edu/~dash/cupid.html

————————————[Attis]————————————

http://www.sacred-texts.com/pag/frazer/gb03400.htm

————————————[Avesta (Zoroastrian texts)]————————————

http://www.avesta.org
http://www.sacred-texts.com/zor/index.htm

————————————[Bible browser in several versions]————————————

http://www.devotions.net/bible/00bible.htm

————————————[the daughters of Danaus]————————————

http://www.mythindex.com/greek-mythology/D/Danaides.html
http://www.paleothea.com/Myths/Danaides.html

————————————[Demeter and Persephone]————————————

http://www.uh.edu/~cldue/texts/demeter.html
http://www.sacred-texts.com/cla/demeter.htm

————————————[Egyptian creation myths]————————————

http://www.sacred-texts.com/egy/index.htm http://www.egyptartsite.com/
crea.html

————————————[Elijah and Elisha]————————————

http://www.jewishvirtuallibrary.org/jsource/biography/Elijah.html

―――――――――――[Enuma Elish]―――――――

http://www.ancient.eu.com/article/225/
http://www.cresourcei.org/enumaelish.html

―――――――――――[Epic of Gilgamesh]――――――

http://www.ancienttexts.org/library/mesopotamian/gilgamesh/

―――――――――――[Hebrew Bible]―――――――

http://www.rosings.com/users/nrsv/nrsvbible.htm#HebrewBible
http://www.devotions.net/bible/00old.htm

―――――――――――[Hermes]―――――――――

http://www.theoi.com/Olympios/HermesMyths.html
http://www.greek-gods.info/greek-gods/hermes/myths/hermes-apollo/

――――――――[Inanna's descent to the underworld]――――――

http://www.sibyllineorder.org/sacred_texts/sw_innana.htm

―――――――――――[Kojiki]―――――――――

http://www.sacred-texts.com/shi/kj/index.htm
http://www.ishwar.com/shinto/holy_kojiki/

―――――――――――[Maui]――――――――――

http://www.sacred-texts.com/pac/grey/grey04.htm
http://www.sacred-texts.com/pac/maui/maui08.htm

―――――――――――[Mahabharata]――――――――

http://www.sacred-texts.com/hin/maha/index.htm
http://www.mahabharataonline.com/translation/index.php

―――――――――――[Metamorphoses]―――――――

http://www.sacred-texts.com/cla/ovid/meta/index.htm
http://etext.virginia.edu/latin/ovid/trans/Ovhome.htm

──────────────{ Orpheus and Eurydice }──────────────

http://www.vcu.edu/engweb/webtexts/eurydice/eurydicemyth.html
http://www.online-mythology.com/orpheus_eurydice/

──────────────{ Osiris & Isis }──────────────

http://www.egyptianmyths.net/mythisis.htm
http://www.philae.nu/philae/IsisOsiris.html

──────────────{ Pan Ku (Pangu) }──────────────

http://www.livingmyths.com/Chinese.htm#Pangu

──────────────{ Prose Edda }──────────────

http://www.sacred-texts.com/neu/pre/index.htm
http://www.cybersamurai.net/Mythology/nordic_gods/LegendsSagas/
    Edda/ProseEdda/ContentsEnglish.htm

──{ Havamal (Norse poetry, Odin's runesong: verse 139) }──

http://oaks.nvg.org/havamal-bellows.html
http://www.cybersamurai.net/Mythology/nordic_gods/LegendsSagas/
    Edda/PoeticEdda/Hovamol.htm#runatal

──────────────{ Rg Veda }──────────────

http://www.sacred-texts.com/hin/rigveda/
http://www.hinduwebsite.com/sacredscripts/rigintro.asp

──────────────{ Sisyphus }──────────────

http://www.greekmythology.com/Books/Odyssey/O_Book_XI/o_book_
    xi.html
http://www.timelessmyths.com/classical/aeolids.html#Sisyphus

──────────────{ Torah }──────────────

http://www.sacred-texts.com/jud/index.htm
http://www.shechem.org/etorahsr.html

────────────[the Vedas]────────────

http://www.sacred-texts.com/hin/
http://www.cincinnatitemple.com/articles/Veda_Books.pdf

────────────[Venus & Adonis]────────────

http://www.online-mythology.com/venus_adonis/
http://avalon100.tripod.com/Venus.html

MYTHICAL CHARACTERS

Achilles: Greek hero of the Trojan War, central character and greatest warrior in Homer's *Iliad.*

Adonis: A handsome youthful man with whom Aphrodite fell in love; killed by a wild boar but later worshipped as a god of vegetation and dying-and-rising god.

Aeneas: Hero of Virgil's *Aeneid,* fought for Troy in the Trojan wars; his descendents founded the city of Rome.

Ahura Mazda: The supreme god of ancient Iranians (Zoroastrians) whose cult was propagated by the legendary prophet Zarathustra; creator of the world, humanity and all that is good.

Ala: Earth mother goddess of the Ibo tribe in Nigeria; creator of the living and queen of the dead; provider of communal loyalty and lawgiver.

Alcyone: Daughter of the wind god, Aeolus; after her husband drowned, they were both turned into winter sea birds.

Amemit (also Ammut, Ammit): A female demon in Egyptian mythology who resides in the underworld; part lion, part hippopotamus, and part crocodile; devourer of all the dead who are judged unworthy of an afterlife.

Amor (also Eros, Cupid): Greek and Roman god of desire, affection and erotic love; son of Venus and Mars.

Angra Mainyu: An evil deity in Zoroastrianism; god of darkness and eternal destroyer of good.

Anshar: A sky god in Akkadian mythology; grandfather of Tiamat and Apsu.

Anu: Akkadian and Sumerian sky god; son of Anshar; god of heaven and lord of constellations.

Anubis: Ancient Egyptian funerary deity; guardian and protector of the dead; portrayed with a black jackal-like head.

Aphrodite (Roman: Venus): Greek goddess of beauty, love, and marriage.

Apollo: Olympian sun god; also god of music, poetry, and medicine; often depicted with a lyre.

Apsu: Primeval Mesopotamian god personifying the sweet waters of the primordial abyss; consort of Tiamat in the Enuma Elish.

Asclepius: Greek god of medicine and healing; killed by Zeus with a lightning bolt for restoring the dead to life; resurrected as a constellation.

Astarte: Eastern Mediterranean goddess; associated with Ishtar, Aphrodite and others; connected with fertility, sexuality and war.

Athena (Roman: Minerva): Greek goddess of wisdom, civilization, warfare, strength, strategy, female arts, justice, and skill; patron deity of Athens.

Attis: In Phrygian and Greek mythology, a demigod associated with vegetation; consort of Cybele, died and was reborn as an evergreen tree.

Basilisk: A legendary reptile known as the king of serpents and believed to cause death with a single glance.

Baubo: An old woman who cheers Demeter while she is mourning the loss of her daughter, Persephone; sometimes understood as a goddess of mirth and bawdy humor.

Behemoth: A mythological beast mentioned in the book of Job; in later Jewish literature the primal unconquerable monster of the land.

Brahma: Hindu god of creation, progenitor of human beings; one of the Trimurti.

Cerberus: In Greek mythology, the three-headed dog who guards the gates of Hades.

Cerridwin: A Celtic shape-shifting goddess and enchantress associated with poetry and wisdom.

Charon: In Greek mythology, the ferryman who carries souls of the recently deceased across the rivers Styx and Acheron that divided the world of the living from the realm of the dead.

Chimera: In Greek mythology, a monstrous female fire-breathing creature with parts composed of various creatures, including the lion, the serpent, and the goat.

Coyote: Trickster god in several Native American traditions; creator and teacher of humans; known for lurking about, causing trouble, and playing pranks.

Cybele: Phrygian earth mother goddess, goddess of caverns, mountains, and fortresses; associated with wild animals, especially lions and bees.

Daughters of Danaus (also Danaids or Danaides): In Greek mythology, the fifty daughters of the king of Argos who obeyed their father's instructions to kill their husbands on their wedding night; condemned to an eternity of labor, carrying jugs of water from the river Styx to fill a bottomless tub.

Demeter (Roman: Ceres): Greek goddess of earth, harvest, and grain; taught humans sowing and ploughing; also a fertility goddess; mother of Persephone.

Dionysus: Greek god of the grape harvest, wine, and wine making; associated with ritual madness and ecstasy; only god to have a mortal parent.

Dumuzi: Sumerian god of vegetation and fertility; shepherd and lord of sheepfolds; husband of Inanna.

Ea: Babylonian god of waters, also crafts, writing, and men's work; one of the three primal gods of Sumer.

Enki: Sumerian equivalent of Ea, often portrayed as a trickster; associated with mischief, sea water, and lake water; patron of the city of Eridu.

Eostre(also Ostara): Attested by Venerable Bede as a Germanic goddess whose name was given to the festival of Easter; sometimes associated with the dawn.

Ereshkigal: Mesopotamian queen of the underworld; the only lawmaker and judge in her kingdom; sister of Inanna; associated with myths symbolizing the change of seasons.

Eris: Greek goddess of strife and discord; believed to haunt battlefields and love bloodshed; set off a chain of events leading to the Trojan War.

Eurydice: In Greek mythology, an oak nymph and wife of Orpheus whose soul entered the underworld after she stepped on a poisonous snake.

Freya (also Freyja): Norse goddess of love and fertility; patron goddess of crops and birth.

Gilgamesh: King of Uruk, a virtuous and brave warrior in Mesopotamian mythology; known for his quest to attain immortality in the Epic of Gilgamesh.

Hades: Brother of Zeus and Poseidon in Greek mythology, king of the underworld and god of death and the dead.

Hecate: Greco-Roman goddess associated with magic, witchcraft, night, the moon, and crossroads as well as nurturing and childbirth; guided Demeter through the night during her search for Persephone.

Heracles (Roman: Hercules): Demigod known for his great strength and for completing the twelve labors; a great warrior but sometimes inclined to cheat.

Hermes (Roman: Mercury): Greek messenger god and guide to the underworld; patron of boundaries and those that cross them; known for his cunning.

Hydra: A many-headed water serpent in Greek mythology.

Inanna: Sumerian goddess of sexual love, fertility, and warfare; called Queen of Heaven.

Ishtar: The Akkadian equivalent of Inanna with a somewhat different mythological narrative.

Isis: Egyptian goddess of motherhood, magic, and fertility; protector of the dead; wife and sister of Osiris and mother of Horus.

Ixion: A Greek king condemned by the gods to suffer an eternity bound to a winged fiery wheel; at first spinning through the heavens but in later myth transferred to Tartarus.

Izanami: Japanese goddess associated with both creation and death; queen of the underworld; wife of Izanagi.

Izanagi: Japanese god born of the seven divine generations; husband and co-creator with Izanami; begetter of Amaterasu, the sun goddess, as well as the gods of moon and storm.

Janus: Roman god of gates, doorways, beginnings, and transitions; most often depicted with two heads facing in opposite directions.

Jason: Mythological hero in classical Greece; famous as leader of Argonauts and their quest for the Golden Fleece.

Jonah: In the Hebrew Bible, a prophet of the northern kingdom of Israel who attempts to flee god by sea, is swallowed by a large fish, repents, and becomes a powerful prophet of God.

Kali: Hindu goddess associated with eternal energy; goddess of time and change; both creator and destroyer.

Krishna: Hindu avatar of Vishnu; a central figure in Hindu mythology, portrayed in many forms, including child-god, prankster, model lover, and supreme being.

Leviathan: Biblical sea monster described in detail in the book of Job.

Lilith: A character of Jewish folklore, said to be the first wife of Adam, created at the same time and of the same earth; also thought to belong to a class of female demons.

Loki: Norse trickster god and shape shifter.

Marduk: Patron deity of the city of Babylon, eventually elevated to supreme deity; destroyer of Tiamat and supreme creator in the *Enuma Elish*.

Maui: Polynesian hero and trickster god; exploits include snaring the sun and creating the Pacific islands.

Michabo: Native American deity known as the Great Hare; Algonquin creator god; associated with the sun and master of thunder and wind.

Mithra: Zoroastrian divinity associated with the sun as well as covenants, oaths, and contracts; also known as a protector of truth; the cult of Mithra ranged from ancient Iranian cultures to Rome and became strongly associated with the Roman army.

Nana: In Phrygian and Greek mythology, Nana was the daughter of a river god; she became impregnated by the divine force in the form of an almond and gave birth to Attis.

Nefertum: An Egyptian solar deity associated with creation stories and symbolized by a blue lotus; also associated with scents and perfumes.

Naga: In India, a class of deity or being taking the form of a great snake, most specifically the King Cobra. The female is a nagi or nagini.

Neti: In Sumerian, Babylonian and Akkadian mythology, a minor underworld god who is chief gatekeeper of the underworld.

Ninshubur: The second-in-command to Inanna in Sumerian mythology. Sometimes called the Queen of the East, she was a goddess in her own right, traveler and messenger for other deities.

Odin: Norse creator god whose name literally means "frenzy," featured in many myths and legends, associated with wisdom, war, poetry, prophecy, and conditions and states that are out of control; sacrificed himself to obtain greater wisdom.

Nut: Egyptian sky goddess, wife and sister of the earth god Geb.

Odysseus (Latin: Ulysses): Hero of Homer's epic, *The Odyssey.* king of Ithaca, known for his ten-year journey home after the Trojan war; also known for devising the stratagem known as the Trojan Horse.

Orpheus: In Greek religion and myth, a legendary musician, poet, and prophet; able to charm all living things with his music; known for his unsuccessful attempt to reclaim his wife, Eurydice, from the underworld.

Osiris: Egyptian deity, husband of Isis, ruler of the underworld and lord of the afterlife; also associated with vegetation and the annual flooding of the Nile.

Pandora: In Greek mythology, the first woman; best known for being unable to contain her curiosity and opening a jar containing all the evils of humankind.

Pan Ku (also Pangu): In Chinese mythology, the first being; a primitive, hairy giant who emerged from a cosmic egg and created the world; when he was laid to rest, parts of his body became all the aspects of nature and humanity.

Penelope: In Homer's *Odyssey,* the faithful wife of Odysseus; famous for her cleverness; practiced deception to keep suitors at bay until her husband returned.

Persephone: Daughter of Zeus and Demeter, goddess of the harvest and queen of the underworld in Greek mythology.

Pomona: Roman goddess of fruitful abundance; keeper of orchards and fruit trees; closely associated with apples.

Poseidon (Roman: Neptune): Greek god of the sea; also associated with earthquakes, protector of many cities.

Psyche: An extraordinarily beautiful woman who appears in an ancient Greek novel by Apuleius; draws the wrath of Aphrodite and becomes the husband of Cupid.

Rahab: Legendary monster of Jewish folklore, dragon of the water, demonic angel of the sea; appears in the book of Isaiah.

Rama: Seventh avatar of Vishnu; one of the most popular figures in Hinduism; husband of Siti, the embodiment of perfect womanhood.

Raven: Native American trickster or culture hero figure known for stealing the sun; creator of the world and of the first people in some narratives.

Re (also Ra): Egyptian god of the sun; creator of all forms of life.

Sakra: In Buddhism, ruler of heaven and lord of the devas; considered one of the protectors of Buddhism.

Semele: In Greek mythology, the lover of Zeus and mortal mother of Dionysus.

Seth: Egyptian god of chaos, also associated with war, deserts, storms, and foreign lands; embodiment of hostility and evil; brother of Osiris and Isis who killed Osiris and tore out the eye of Horus.

Sisyphus: A mortal Greek king condemned to Tartarus by the gods for his hubris (mortal arrogance); condemned to roll a boulder up a steep hill for eternity.

Siva: One of the Trimurti in the Hindu tradition, the destroyer, and transformer.

Sol Invictus: The unconquerable sun, official sun god of the later Roman Empire.

Tammuz: Babylonian and Sumerian god of food and vegetation; possibly derived from the earlier Sumerian deity, Dumuzi.

Tantalus: A Greek mortal ruler condemned to eternal deprivation of nourishment in Tartarus for sacrificing his son and serving his flesh as food for the gods.

Tara: A female buddha or bodhisattva known as the mother of liberation; a tantric meditation deity in Tibetan Buddhism.

Telemachus: In Greek mythology, the son of Odysseus and Penelope; a central character in the Odyssey, known for his journeys seeking news of his father.

Tiamat: Primordial ocean goddess, conquered by Marduk who created heaven and earth from her body; mother of all; also a chaos monster.

Toth: Egyptian deity associated with magic, writing, and judgment of the dead; sometimes considered the heart and tongue of the sun god, Ra; often depicted with the head of an ibis or a baboon; animals are sacred to him.

Typhon: Most deadly of all monsters in Greek mythology; called the father of all monsters; finally defeated by Zeus.

Uzume: Japanese goddess of happiness and joy, also known for trickery; in Shinto religion, the goddess of happiness, revelry, and dawn.

Vishnu: One of the Trimurti in the Hindu tradition, the maintainer, and preserver.

Vrtra: Hindu chaos monster taking the form of a serpent or dragon; kept the waters captive until slain by Indra.

Yam: Ugaritic god of rivers and the sea; deity of primordial chaos representing the power of the sea.

Ymir: Norse frost giant and founder of a race of frost giants; Odin and his
brothers killed him and created the universe from parts of his body.

Zephyr: Greek god of the gentle west wind; messenger of spring.

Zeus (Roman: Jupiter): Greek father of the gods, ruler of the Olympian deities; god of sky and thunder.

GLOSSARY

Aboriginal: Original or earliest known (see primal cultures).

Abrahamic faiths: The world's three primary monotheistic religions: Judaism, Christianity, and Islam.

Ad'ham: Hebrew term meaning humankind.

Ad'hama: Hebrew term meaning dust or earth.

Anthropomorphism: The attribution of human characteristics to a non-human entity such as a deity.

Arbitrary symbol: Also called a conventional symbol; a symbol that is culturally determined, its meaning dependent upon its context.

Archetype: A prototype symbol or pattern of behavior upon which others are copied or based. In Jungian psychology, the term refers to a collectively inherited unconscious idea, pattern of thought, image, etc., universally present in individual psyches, that channels experiences and emotions.

Avatar: The deliberate manifestation of a deity in bodily form. The term is primarily applied to manifestations of the Hindu deity Vishnu, although other deities are sometimes associated with the term.

The Axial Age: A phrase coined by Karl Jaspers referring to the period between approximately 800 and 200 BCE during which a concentration of new and different religious beliefs emerged in different parts of the world, including China, Greece, India, and the Middle East.

Bara: A Hebrew Biblical term used to refer to God's acts of creation, sometimes erroneously translated as creation out of nothing.

Bardo: A Tibetan term literally meaning intermediate state, the state of existence between incarnations; the passage of consciousness from the physical body into a transitional state.

Bodhisattva: One who is on the path to enlightenment. In Mahayana Buddhism, the term may refer to one who has attained full realization but compassionately postpones final enlightenment in order to assist others on the path. The primary characteristics of a bodhisattva are wisdom and compassion.

Collective unconscious: In Jungian psychology, the inborn unconscious psychic material common to humankind, accumulated through the experience of all preceding generations.

Cosmogony: A narrative explaining the origins of life and the coming into existence of the universe.

Cosmology: The study of the universe and humanity's place in it.

Creatrix: A female creator.

Dark matter: An invisible form of matter inferred to exist based on observation of gravitational effects on visible matter and background radiation. Based on the mass-density of ordinary matter, dark matter may constitute 80 to 90 percent of the matter in the universe.

Discursive symbols: Singular symbols appearing in linear or discrete units whose meanings depend on a particular order or arrangement.

Duat: The ancient Egyptian underworld; the realm through which Egyptians passed after death.

Etiological Myth: A myth whose purpose is to explain the origins of social or natural phenomena.

Figure-ground perception: A term used in gestalt perception theory referring to the innate human tendency to perceive in terms of a figure (the object in focus) and a ground (the background or setting which fills the rest of the scene).

Fixity: An intrinsic quality of ritual referring to fixed times and places of ritual practice and repetition at specific intervals.

Gehenna: A word used by Rabbinical and early Christian cultures to refer to the underworld region where the wicked go to be punished.

Hades (or *Erebus*): The Greek word used both to refer to the underworld and to its ruler.

Heisenberg's uncertainty principle: A principle in quantum mechanics having to do with certain physical properties such as position and momentum; the consequence of the principle is that the more precisely one of the two properties is measured, the less precisely the other property can be measured.

Henotheism: Religious systems that worship only one supreme deity without denying the existence of other deities that may be validly worshipped.

Hierophanic symbol: A symbol that serves to manifest the sacred in the world.

Iconic symbol: A pictorial or geometric representation.

***Jataka* tales:** Ancient collections of stories narrating the Buddha's life experiences before his last human incarnation.

Kur: The Sumerian term for underworld, referring to the void space between the primeval sea and the earth that served as the home of the dead. The term may also refer to land or mountain.

Matriarchal Culture: A culture in which females rather than males are in positions of primary leadership and/or reverence.

Me: In Sumerian myth, universal decrees of divine authority that make civilization possible. *Me* are fundamental to the Sumerian understanding of the relationship between the gods and humanity.

Monolatrism: Recognition of the existence of several gods while holding one god as singularly worthy of worship.

Monomyth: A term used by Joseph Campbell referring to a fundamental mythic pattern upon which other classic myths are based; also referred to as the "hero's journey."

Multivocality: Literally "many voices", the capacity of symbols to carry multiple meanings and to represent different meanings to different groups and individuals.

Paleolithic: Referring to the second part of the Stone Age beginning approximately 750,000 to 500,000 BCE, and ending with the end of the Ice Age about 8,500 BCE.

Pantheon: All collective gods and goddesses of a particular people or religion.

Paradigm shift: A change in fundamental assumptions within the dominating theory.

Paschal: Of, or relating to, Passover or Easter.

Pesach: Hebrew and Yiddish term for the Jewish festival known as Passover, commemorating the liberation of the Hebrew people from slavery in Egypt.

Polytheism: The belief and worship of multiple gods or goddesses.

Primal culture: An alternative term for cultures with a mythic worldview, an interconnected relationship with the natural and spiritual world and a strong identification with community. Although these cultures typically have ancient origins, a few such cultures continue to exist.

Presentational symbol: A symbol containing multiple components that must be perceived as a whole to determine its meaning.

Primordial: existing at the very beginning; original; elementary.

Psyche: Greek word for soul. The psyche comprises the soul, self, and mind and refers to all the forces in an individual that influence thought, behavior, and personality.

Rite of passage: A ritual marking the progression from one status to another, typically marking milestones in life when major transitions occur.

Samhain (also Samuin): Summer's End, a Celtic or Gaelic harvest festival considered by some to mark the Celtic new year; also celebrated as a religious festival by some neopagans.

Samsara: The karmic cycle of life, death, and rebirth.

Saturnalia: An ancient Roman festival celebrated around the time of the winter solstice in honor of Saturn (Cronus), father of the major Greek and Roman deities.

Shakti: Primordial cosmic energy; also the concept or personification of divine female power; responsible for creation and the agent of all change.

Shamanism: Beliefs and practices involving healing techniques, typically including communication with the spirit world. A shaman acts as a medium between the natural and spirit worlds in order to provide healing to the individual and the community.

Sheol: Hebrew for grave or pit, the underworld, the place where the dead gather.

Tanniyn (also tannin, tanninim): Hebrew term for sea or river monster, also sometimes translated as whale, serpent, or dragon.

Tartarus: In later Greek mythology, a deep pit or abyss lying beneath the underworld, serving as a place of torment, suffering, and punishment.

Tehom: In Hebrew, the Deep or Abyss; the primordial state of chaos prior to creation.

Totem: An Ojibwa term referring to an object, usually an animal or plant, that serves as the emblem of a family, clan, or community; sometimes considered an ancestor or spirit guide; sometimes used in contemporary culture to refer to an individual's spirit guide or emblem.

Trimurti: The three forms of the divine in the Hindu tradition: Brahma, Vishnu, and Siva.

Ubuntu (also *botho*): African concept of communal identity—a human being is a person through interaction with other people, sometimes translated as "I am because we are."

Void: Nothingness; formlessness.

Xibalba: The Mayan underworld—a terrifying realm where the dead face torture and suffering.

Yomi: The Japanese underworld—a land of gloom and shadows where the dead reside in perpetuity; ruled over by Izanami.